You Don't
Know Jack

You Don't Know Jack

ALISA M MURPHY

AS TOLD BY
FRANK J MATTHEWS

ISBN: 1517651387
ISBN 13: 9781517651381

Dedicated to Thomas Michael Murphy, who believed in me, believed in Jack, and championed us with practical support and genuine enthusiasm through this entire process.

Author's Preface

So many titles came to mind over the years that I worked on this book. Days spent quietly sitting and listening to my Uncle Jack recount his life stories led me towards book titles both grand and plain, provocative and proletariat.

Some of the titles I considered were inspired by the truly unique American nature of his journey and hence brought to mind sweeping themes of grand Americana...*An American Life...The American Man*..... not quite wrong, but not quite right either. Several possibilities hinted of nostalgia for times gone by, a look at our past as it were......*Across the Generations* - No, too PBS special. *The Decades*... sounds more like a soap opera... moving on. Next came the military inspired titles. These were hard to escape given my protagonist's lifetime of service to the stars and stripes; and who doesn't love a Marine after all. Maybe *A Semper Fi Life*...hmmm...this isn't just a war story. And of course there was the music. Alas, musical titles just didn't do it… music went with Jack on his journey, always there, always being formed and maneuvered in his mind. Music was a companion providing the accompaniment to each of life's twists and turns. But ultimately the music alone did not dictate his path.

So in searching for the perfect title I considered carefully what I wanted from this book. I wanted Jack's story to be known, to be appreciated, to inspire. The truth is that all around us are incredible life stories that we never learn. The stories of men and women who go about their daily lives doing things that are truly remarkable and that we never know about.

In our current culture I see notoriety too frequently confused with actual achievement. Fame now attempts to take the place of real accomplishment. Outlandish behavior draws more attention than honor. Reverence is often given out on the basis of celebrity and not as a result of distinction.

In fact, some among us are driven by little more than a desire to be "famous." In this pursuit they usually decide to skip the years of hard work and sacrifice it would take to invent a treatment that could cure disease, or be part of a history-making NASA launch team. Instead they opt to do or say something ridiculous, take off their clothes, or make a scene to achieve notoriety. How fortuitous for them that our current society makes this route to success so accessible. Suddenly, without toil, study, or actual achievement, the whole western universe will do just about anything to hear their thoughts, or learn about the minutia of their daily lives. These individuals become the ones who are celebrated by society, even venerated.

Meanwhile, this world is bursting with men like Jack-the hard-working, the honest, and the courageous. As unknowns they remain uncelebrated. Their stories are never recognized by more than a handful of friends and family. When studied more closely, these anonymous lives are pretty remarkable. For instance, my late Grandfather: born into extreme poverty he endured working the rough life of the carnival as a mere child, survived horrific injuries sustained in a high-rise construction accident, worked in the oil boom of Pennsylvania, and could build a bike or a lawn mower from a few rusty parts and a paper clip a la MacGyver style. Or my father, who, despite a valiant fight, lost his family farm to the Government land grab for the Kinzua Dam. He went on to drive a tank in the Army, and then substantially more harrowing…drove a school bus for over thirty years. He got thousands of kids to and from school safely, in snowstorms and blue skies, without acknowledgment or recognition beyond a simple man's paycheck. Or my friend Dan, a literal walking encyclopedia of cars;

a lifelong motorhead who worked in factories building the machines that have created giant turbines and jet engines. Will his vast knowledge of Mopars and machining land him on a Red Carpet, bulbs flashing and champagne flowing?…most assuredly, no.

So while vacuous women in various stages of undress, musicians with drug problems, abusive athletes, and anyone that manages to get on a reality show, will invariably secure the trappings of notoriety in America, most men and women will go on as stars only of their own lives. They will remain the unknown and unsung heroes in the cubicles, labs, garages, and stores of America; the nursing home caregiver, the transmission mechanic, the air conditioner repairman, the dental assistant and yes, a man like Jack. So…You Don't Know Jack. Finally, the title I was looking for had arrived.

I hope that this story will not only inspire you to consider the life of this one remarkable man, but to consider the lives of the men and women that surround you every day. Consider everything that makes them the extraordinary individuals they are, and to learn their unique life stories. In the end, I hope that they will each become famous…at least to those who love them.

A.M.M.

When sunset lights the purple skies,
Which day from darkness divide…
Far away in the East where the moon will rise,
There's a bugle call – In the Eveningtide.

PFC Frank Jackson Matthews
Iwo Jima, March 16, 1945

One

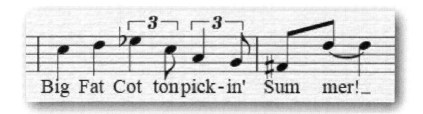

Frank Jackson Matthews
Big Fat Cotton-Picking Summer

T he church filled steadily with the sounds of whispering voices and friendly greetings spoken in hushed
tones. From his seat behind a small folding organ, in the
shadow of an imposing wooden podium, Jack watched
as the crowd slowly filed in. His fingers deftly played the
popular hymn, *Softly and Tenderly,* with equal amounts of
precision and ease. He knew the piece so well that as his
hands worked the keys, and his feet worked the pedals,

he could look about the room and study the growing group of congregants.

The men removed their hats as they passed through the broad doors of the sunlit sanctuary. Women in their finest summer dresses, with their hands ensconced in white gloves, clutched family Bibles. A few children, who were not much younger than Jack's twelve years, were clustered in the back corners and they chattered amongst themselves excitedly. Now and again a stern faced mother shushed them severely and they reluctantly shuffled into seats near their respective parents.

The discreet prattling continued unabated for nearly twenty minutes and bits and pieces of the conversations floated to Jack's ears...

"Did you hear...?"

"It's a shame about the ...."

"Lord sakes what did Hazel say about it...?"

"I don't believe the President will ever..."

The sanctuary grew warmer as the crowd multiplied and the South Carolina sun beat down on the fields surrounding the rapidly filling Presbyterian church.

From the side of a long row of wooden pews, Jack's father strode confidently toward the center of the dais. A striking figure of a man, he was dressed in a stiff dark suit and a crisp white shirt with a small striped bow tie encircling the starched collar. His gray eyes were focused and serious behind a small pair of oval framed glasses. His face was an intelligent one - not particularly kind in nature - but certainly it conveyed a strong sense of dignity and command. By the time he took the few steps to the center front of the church all individual conversations had promptly ceased and a hush fell across the fervent congregation.

Expectant faces gazed forward in full and rapt attention completely directed toward the man at center stage. A Presbyterian Minister, Jack's father would hold revivals in small churches like this one across the rural south, always dragging his young son with him to provide the music. His father would preach and Jack would do his best to get a decent volume of sound from whatever small packable organ or piano was available.

He was a natural on the instruments and exceedingly proficient for his age, which was always to the surprise and delight of the crowd. Mothers beamed at the young prodigy and fathers nodded their heads in approval and wondered silently why their sons couldn't be more like the slender and serious-faced twelve-year-old sitting behind the piano.

* * *

Jack had been born Frank Jackson Matthews in 1926 in the small town of Preston, Georgia, to mother Mary Lee Doster and father Curtis Jackson Matthews.

Mary had met Curtis in Congregationalist Seminary, married the young minister, and settled into the role of housewife. Soon she was mother to baby "Jack," as the family called him, and his younger sister, June.

Father Curtis Jackson Matthews was a stoic and reserved man and a competent minister. Being much disciplined and serious, he was well suited to be named after the Confederate hero and notorious stoic, General Stonewall Jackson. It could be said that Curtis was generally a man more focused on providing a good and moral education to young Jack than any overt fatherly kindness.

As a toddler, baby Jack's constitution was tested and strengthened by bouts with Typhoid, Diphtheria, and just about every other illness that a child could contract. When he was seven, the family moved to Newberry, South Carolina. Father Curtis had been assigned to pastor not just one, but three Presbyterian churches in the area. As there was no frequency of Congregational churches in the South, Curtis had made the practical decision to convert to the Presbyterian faith. The denomination's leadership would move the minister to wherever he was needed to lead a flock, or flocks, as it were.

Newberry was a typical, small southern town, situated half-way between Columbia and Greenville in the central Piedmont district of the state. Outside of the handful of streets that comprised the rural community, the surrounding countryside was a mixture of forests, farms, and rivers. The Matthews family lived in the parsonage house next to one of the assigned churches and the pastor served that congregation as well as those of its two sister churches located on the town's peripheries.

It was here in this small country town that Jack began receiving piano lessons from a local woman for $1.50 a month. He practiced what he learned on the old beat-up piano in the church next door where his father was the assigned minister. The church, like the Matthews home, did not have electricity and it was a cold and shadowy place outside of normal service hours. Jack was always sent alone to practice in the eerie basement underneath the dark and empty sanctuary. He would shudder a bit and cling tightly to the small kerosene lamp that allowed him just enough dim light to see the piano's yellowing and cracked keys. The more he practiced the more his natural gift revealed itself, and by the age of twelve Jack's piano skills were finer than any adult for miles around.

So, with his son to assist him, Curtis Matthews preached the gospel every week at the three separate churches, and traveled regularly to preach revivals whenever and wherever he was invited.

The revivals would generally include two full services each day for a week during which time the father and son would board with a local family. Jack was not simply along for the utilitarian purpose of providing music, but for the draw he would provide. Fliers would advertise the upcoming revival with the guest preacher and his young accomplished musician. Jack's budding talent provided an element of interest and excitement to each event. So now, with the summer revival season in full swing, Jack played, his father preached, and so it went from town to town and church to church. The travel was always a welcome break from his usual routine of school and studying. Even better, it was another chance to be out of the house and away from the tensions of his parent's marriage.

On an elementary level Jack felt the love and attachment to both of his parents that came naturally to any child. But as he grew he felt something else as well. The feeling was best described as sympathy. From a young age he realized that as individuals, and hence as a couple, his parents were disappointingly flawed. No one paid the price for these flaws more than each other. Jack observed that his parent's interactions were brief, perfunctory, and devoid of any tenderness or demonstrable love.

Father Curtis Matthews had grown up in near poverty conditions in the mountains of North Georgia. His people were modest mountain folk who lived in and around the Appalachians and had little in the way of material possessions or societal status. His simple country upbringing had done nothing to temper the strict and governing nature that was a large part of his personality.

In sharp contrast, Mother Mary Matthews came from relative wealth and an ancestry that could claim both significant valuable land holdings and a noble line of genetics. Mary's parents were both deceased at a young age and she was raised by a strict and dour Grandmother who reminded the young girl on a regular basis that just about everything in life was sinful. It seemed to Jack that his great grandmother had imparted on his mother a notion of a dreary and grim God who shunned joy in any form. Mother had her good points. To her credit she was efficient, practical, and hard-working. She always made certain the children and the congregation had what they needed, when they needed it.

Certainly life had dealt her a fair share of challenges. Enduring the loss of both parents and the loss of two infant children along the way could not have been easy. Possibly the inability to apply her own seminary education to any meaningful occupation may have been a contributing source of unhappiness. Whether through upbringing, or circumstance, or just the nature of her personality, his mother became what young Jack recognized as a belly-aching complainer. She was rarely pleased with any aspect of life and was an unsupportive wife who criticized Curtis at every turn.

It did not escape his notice that father spent the majority of his time at the church office, away from the harsh tongue and disapproving looks of his nagging wife. The benefits of this technique were not lost on the preacher's young progeny and Jack learned quickly how to stay away from the home himself. When he was young he kept to his studies and the church piano. At times he would work in the school library where he felt at home among the stacks of books and at peace away from his mother's continual complaints. He resolved at a young age that he would not be a man driven to avoidance of his own home and family. He would never marry someone with a sour disposition or joyless approach to daily life.

Admittedly the childhood of Frank Jackson Matthews was not a typical childhood, but Jack was not a typical child of his era. In fact he was distinctly different. While most boys his age were concerned with sneaking cigarettes or drinking beer, he was dreaming of academic achievement. When he wasn't practicing piano he was usually concerned with his own educational development. The county had a mobile library and once a week, every week, he would make a selection of several books and read them through voraciously.

The books were about everything and anything that he could imagine – science, history, literature… and *especially* music. Jack would drink thirstily from their pages every bit of knowledge they could serve up. He was exceptionally more interested in world news, philosophy, and the progress of academics than he was in pilfering a Chesterfield from some fellas pop.

Reading wasn't a mere matter of curiosity or escape; in his mind he was planning for the day he would teach at a major university. Of course, his parents assumed he would attend seminary and become a man of religious teaching, but Jack's desire was to teach music. To work in the heart of knowledge, to impact young minds like his own, to be surrounded by music, and theory, and books… that seemed like a world that he wanted to exist in. That was a world that he wanted to be his future.

To become a university teacher would require a master's degree and Jack knew getting a degree like that would require money. The Matthews family always had food on the table but their means were meager. The modest pay of a preacher, a mere $550 a year, would not allow Jack's father to pay for an expensive education. So, even as he watched each faith-filled and Sunday-dressed crowd fill the sanctuaries, he wondered over and over where he would get it from.

TWO

When I'm look-ing for a band, I like to start with Dix-ie-land!

Frank Jackson Matthews
Look Away to the Dixieland Band

The year 1940 began with the world in flames. From his bedroom in the backwoods of South Carolina Jack listened intently to the news on his tiny Philco radio. The radio had been a gift for his thirteenth birthday and now served as his ears to the world. At the moment it was bringing him the continuing reports of Hitler's conquests in Europe.

As the German tyrant continued to take control of greater and greater expanses of that faraway continent, it seemed that no one, other than maybe Britain's Churchill, was going to stand in his way. One by one the leaders of European countries were feigning neutrality, bending to Hitler's will, or completely surrendering. In Asia, the Japanese were advancing in solidifying their physical and political control of almost all of mainland China, the Eastern Asian countries, and their island neighbors. Stalin's Soviet Red Army had invaded Poland, and Italy's Mussolini, with its impressive naval power, had signed on to join Germany's Axis. In Newberry, South Carolina, life went on much as it always had.

Jack's Philco radio brought something even more compelling than the news…it brought music.

Late at night he would lie in his bed looking out the window, listening to music and watching the moonlit windmill turn in the family's yard. The windmill pumped and stored water for the new bathroom that father Curtis had built on the end of the home's front porch.

Jack kept the radio's volume low so as not to wake up his sister in the next room. He noticed that somehow the music seemed to come in clearer at night. He would listen to WLW from Cincinnati or WWL from New Orleans. Each night would end the same; eventually his mother, with her ever-sharp ears, would come in and turn off the radio for the night. Jack would close his eyes tightly and pretend to be asleep to avoid another lecture about bedtime. He and his mother both knew this was a ruse. He would never fall asleep during music. Music was so precious that the need for sleep could never eclipse it.

Even with the radio turned off, his mind continued to play music. He would re-play and then re-compose the sounds in his mind, always thinking of ways the pieces could be improved. Sometimes it was by rearranging them, other times it was by adding instruments or changing the refrains.

His favorite classical piece at the moment was Cesar Franck's, *D-Minor Symphony*. Listening to his radio had taught him that France was in great peril and the particularly somber sounds of the piece seemed appropriate to the times.

When in a lighter mood, he would listen to Tommy Dorsey songs. Dorsey was the reigning king of the trombone and Jack could play all of his current hits on the upright piano. He happily composed song after song in the Dorsey style and carefully documented them in his manuscript book. For him it was a fun exercise, but also a very private one. He couldn't imagine showing his songs to his piano teacher; she was much more concerned with his practice schedule than his creativity. Maybe someday he would send them to Mr. Dorsey... no, he would keep them private.

In the spring, Jack's piano teacher put him to work learning the theme and variations by Beethoven of Paisiello's, *La Molinara*. Not content with simply memorizing the piece, Jack dissected and analyzed it to see how Beethoven had put it together. It was soon apparent to him that key to such an epic composition was to create a theme that was so bland in nature that the variations could take on lives of their own. He created the assigned theme in a most simplistic form and then fashioned variations for the clarinet. Benny Goodman was the current clarinet idol and one whose music moved easily between the classical and the popular. Jack wrote a piece that was also something of both these styles. For his teacher, he completed the exercise very simply for clarinet and piano, but privately he heard it with a full rich orchestra.

He never told the teacher about either the dissection he had done or of the more elaborate orchestrations he envisioned. She seemed pleased with the simple theme and that was enough to move on.

In the summers Jack always left Newberry and worked at Montreat, the seasonal sanctuary for Presbyterian ministers. Montreat was situated in a beautiful cove of forest and streams in the Blue Ridge Mountains of Western, North Carolina. The retreat had a central Inn, a large lake, nature trails, and a variety of residential cottages. For the visiting ministers it was a time of fellowship, as well as spiritual and physical renewal. For Jack, and other young boys who worked there, it was a time to clean rooms and mop floors. He didn't mind the work – after all, it was a chance to be away from home – but the best part of summer at Montreat was the music lessons. During his very first summer there he had been introduced to Mrs. Crosby Adams. Mrs. Adams was a highly acclaimed music teacher who had moved to Montreat in the supposed waning years of her life. There she lived in a peaceful cottage called, *House-In-the-Woods*, where she continued to teach music and host music teachers from around the country. Upon hearing Jack play the piano she immediately took him under her wing and began weekly lessons. She was a kind and most encouraging instructor with what Jack recognized as the finest of skills as both a composer and a teacher. It was in those summer tutorials with Mrs. Adams that he advanced his talent to another echelon and began to master the art of composition.

By the fall of 1941 his Newberry piano teacher had progressed from Beethoven and now had Jack learning the *First Arabesque* by French composer Claude Debussy. At that moment Jack was more interested in the trumpet playing of Harry James than in the classical impressionist compositions of Debussy. Harry James had an elegance in his playing that Jack held in high regard. Away from the eyes of his teacher, he combined the classical skills he was learning with the blues style he admired. Within the pages of his private music book he composed an airy and elegant song in the combined

style of both musicians and called it, *Arabesque In Blue.*
It was a sophisticated and graceful piece of music that
spoke to him now and promised to come to mind over
and over as the years went by.

And of course, he didn't show it to anyone.

Three

I saw in-side the boy he was   the man that he would be.

Frank Jackson Matthews
Anthem for Bar-Mitzvah

O n one mild December South Carolina afternoon, fifteen-year-old Jack was meandering outside his father's church among the crowd of congregants. They were stretching their legs and gossiping about local events during the brief recess between the formal service and church fellowship time.

Nearby a slender, middle-aged man, stood against his car door and listened intently to the crackled transmissions of his radio. The shiny black car was a 1940

Packard and the pride of its owner being both the newest car for miles around and representing many years of sacrifice on the part of the delighted gentleman who was now its master. Jack couldn't help but admire the car from where he stood leaning against the base of a large pecan tree.

Suddenly the man let out an audible whoop, and leaving the door of the prized car standing ajar, ran hollering into the front of the sanctuary. Within minutes the news raced through the church, inside and out, that Pearl Harbor had been attacked by the Japanese. That night the congregants of Newberry's Presbyterian churches sat listening intently to their radios for even the smallest bits of news about the attack. What had happened? What would the President say? What would we do about it? And, the overriding question in each mind…how many battleships were lost?

Everyone was thirsty for information. Even the boys who normally couldn't be bothered with something as boring as the news eagerly gathered around groups of talking adults to listen in silent and wide-eyed rapt attention to the latest developments.

It would be several days before the fog of rumors and initial reports would finally and clearly reveal that nine battleships of the Pacific fleet were damaged or sunk in the Hawaiian harbor. The vessels that were submerged included the *USS Arizona, USS West Virginia,*

USS Oklahoma, and the *USS California.* Damaged, but remaining above water, were the *USS Tennessee, USS Maryland, USS Pennsylvania,* and the *USS Nevada.* The training ship and veteran of World War I, the *USS Utah* was also downed in the attack. Beyond the battleships another eleven smaller vessels - including several destroyers, cruisers, and a minelayer - were damaged or lost, as were 328 aircraft. Most devastating was the loss of life, with 2,403 Americans killed in the brief, but horrendous, one hour and fifteen-minute attack.

The impacts of war now came to America, even to the small country towns of South Carolina. In nearby Columbia the recruiting offices signed up young men to fight for Uncle Sam against the great tyrants of Europe and Asia. With the arrival of the recruiters also came the news of the GI bill and Jack's mind danced as he saw a way to get the university education he dreamed of.

During the next summer at Montreat Jack discussed his plan with his mentor, Mrs. Crosby Adams. Mrs. Adams thought it a sensible plan and suggested that Jack always carry a supply of music composition paper with him wherever he went while in the military. She had said: "It will force you to compose music without relying on a piano."

With his plan now in place, Jack waited out the hands of time for the moment in June 1943 when he would be seventeen and old enough to join the military with a parent's signature. The only wrinkle in Jack's military to university plan was his father, who flatly refused to let him join the service. Normally there would have been the hope of being randomly drafted, but father Curtis Matthews, as a local community leader, was on the draft board and had openly stated he would prevent Jack from ever making it onto those potentially deadly rolls.

Unwilling to give up, Jack hitched a ride to the recruiters office in Columbia and secured a set of permission papers, worthless as they were without a signature. He squirreled them away at home in a dark recess of a chifforobe drawer and waited in patient anticipation of his parent's next marital divide.

Finally the day came when his father had done something or other to get mother very angry with him. In that perfect moment of spousal discord Jack hurriedly produced the papers and his mother readily signed them. Jack slapped on the three cent stamp he had been holding in reserve and ran them to the mailbox. He was going to be a Marine.

Four

the boy he was is put a way,

Frank Jackson Matthews
Anthem for Bar-Mitzvah

In the sweltering heat of July 1943 Jack climbed on a bus headed south for Parris Island and basic-training camp. The regimented nature of boot camp suited him and he seemed to accomplish each task assigned to him with ease. The boys brought in from the North struggled and bellyached incessantly about the heat. Compared to the stagnant and oppressive humidity of inland South Carolina, Jack found the sea breezes of Parris Island to be rather pleasant.

A month into training he had the misfortune of stepping on a nail and being given a second tetanus shot only a month after his initial inoculation. The double dose of vaccine caused an unfortunate reaction, and with a 104 degree fever he performed only at the marksman level on his shooting test. This was much poorer than his self-perceived skill level - after all, his mother had taught him how to fire a rifle at the age of six.

Mary Matthews was forever in fear that the family's life in the rural south, combined with Curtis's long hours away from home, would make the young mother and her two children easy targets for tramps and other no-goods that might be making their way through the countryside. She herself was a crack shot and she was darn sure going to be certain that her oldest child also had the appropriate skills for protecting the family. For his part, Jack enjoyed shooting and over the years he brought home many a squirrel for the family dinner table. By his early teens he was what the neighboring men described as, "a damn good shot." So it was a great personal disappointment to the young recruit that in his weakened condition he only achieved an average marksman designation.

Other than the small scar on his arm, and the small scar on his pride, he recovered his health and completed his training uneventfully.

When he had first boarded that bus for Parris Island, he wondered if the Marine Corps would mean the end of music in his life. He needn't have worried. Even as a raw recruit, the minister's son was sought out by every chaplain along the way. There was always a service of some kind that needed accompaniment - Protestant or Catholic – piano or organ. Everywhere he went it seemed a chaplain was waiting to shove a schedule of services into his hand. Somehow the chaplains always knew how to find him; Jack hoped the military's intelligence services were even half as good.

From Parris Island he was moved on in his training to Camp Lejeune, North Carolina, then to Quantico, Virginia. Finally, late in 1944, he was loaded onto a troop train headed for Camp Pendleton, California. En route the train stopped briefly in Algiers, Louisiana. It was a sunny September morning and the recruits stood on the bank of the Mississippi river and looked across its wide expanses to the glittering skyline of New Orleans. The city had always drawn Jack like a siren's song. Maybe it was those years of listening to WWL, or knowing that New Orleans was a place filled with so many talented musicians and such a variety of music. Now he was so close, and yet impossibly far, to his personal version of the *emerald city.* There on the bank of the mighty river, Jack and the other Marines performed their calisthenics on a vast bed of thousands of white oyster shells before re-boarding their west-bound train.

Soon he was settling into Camp Pendleton for his final days of training. Here in faraway California he was as distant from his native south as he had ever been both in geography and in his life circumstance. California was a beautiful place; the wildness of the green mountains running down to the blue of the sea stirred his mind. As had always been the case for Jack, the sounds of music flowed in and out of his thoughts. Notes, chords, and the reverberations of individual instruments spiraled with ease around everything he was seeing and feeling as if he spoke a second language of notes and tempos with fluency.

For a time the rush of training had not allowed him to contemplate anything beyond the next challenge. During those days his mind and body had certainly never slowed down enough to physically pen the flats and sharps of music. Now, sitting in his tent alone, just days from Christmas, his mind reeled with how his life had changed so dramatically from that of a simple studious southern boy to a Marine.

Humming softly he picked up a pencil and began to write in his music composition book. Yes, he had taken the advice of Mrs. Crosby Adams, - now where he went, the book went also. No one seemed to notice his book, or his writing. Marines generally didn't notice any private first class, especially scrawny eighteen-year-old, "*feather merchants,*" as they frequently referred to them. His tent mate was a guy from Brooklyn named Dunetz who never asked about or commented on Jack's continual scribbling, even when they were on maneuvers in the wilderness. Jack figured that Brooklyn guys had probably seen just about everything.

Here in these foreign circumstances, the act of composing music took him home...home to a place in his mind that was as familiar to him as if he were back working in stacks of books at the school library, or playing the piano at Montreat, or sitting in front of a congregation in a South Carolina church. Page after page of lined paper filled steadily with the written representation of rhythms and tempos that had taken on life and form in the synapses of his mind throughout his journey as Marine Recruit Matthews. The seemingly simple action of scribbling notes onto paper brought him a great sense of contentment and order...a sense of peace.

He recalled with some annoyance the very first song he had ever written. He was twelve years old and with all the pride of a cat bringing home a mouse, he had brought the song into the kitchen to show his mother. The reaction she gave him was similar to the one she had given the mouse carrying cat.

"That's a love song!" she exclaimed with equal amounts of surprise and derision as if he had handed her a severed rodent head and not a piece of composition paper. "Write about something you know," she had scolded.

So, Jack wrote a song about springtime.

Now the private sat in his tent alone and once again his mind turned to matters of the heart. His mother had been right; he didn't know anything about love. His time in the Marines had done nothing to change that. Still, he was moved to write a song about *anticipated* love and he called it, *I Wonder Who's Waiting for Me*. It was a simple and naïve piece that became more sophisticated and complex as it moved along; Jack guessed this was a lot like love.

The wistful moments of reflection at Camp Pendleton didn't last. The men soon boarded a transport ship bound for Pearl Harbor where the private was destined to take his place among the 4th Division Marines. The trip took several days and in the evenings the men gathered on deck to watch variety-show style movies that had been put together for them in Hollywood. On one particular evening it had rained and the deck of the ship was wet and cold. The movie that night included a song and dance number by Lena Horne. Jack thought that despite the weather, he could probably stay out there and watch her all night long. The stunning songstress was singing something called the *Brazilian Boogie*. Unfortunately, to Jack's ear it was neither Brazilian, nor a boogie. The lyrics claimed the *"power of a puma"*…something the song *didn't* have, but that he was certain Lena did. He pulled out his music sketch book and for the next couple days he composed what he considered to be better pieces of music for the chanteuse. One was a Gershwin style torch song called, *When Love is Gone,* and the other was an upbeat number he titled, *Things are Looking Up for Me.* By the time the ship pulled into Pearl Harbor Jack had Lena all fixed up with better songs, whether she knew it or not. And of course…he never sent them to her.

Five

Frank Jackson Matthews
The Bells of New Years
Written Shipboard, USS Sanborn, 1945
"Where the bells of New Year's existed
only in my imagination."

The Hawaiian Islands were every bit the paradise that Jack had read about in books back in the school library. He felt a surge of invigoration as the exotic sights and sounds of the islands mixed in his senses like the rums and fruits of a smooth, cool, tropical drink.

There was no illusion that he was there on vacation. His shorn hair reminded him every time he looked in a mirror that he was going to war. Still, his youthful interpretation of the war was as little more than the opportunity for adventure. Anything different from daily life in sleepy, rural South Carolina seemed patently exotic.

From the bustling island of Oahu Jack and the other marines were transported on an overnight steamer to Kahului Harbor in Maui. The trip should have been a thoroughly unremarkable one but for the unfortunate occurrence of especially rough inter-island swells. What semblance of a Christmas celebration dinner they had been given in Oahu was invariably refunded to the sea from whence it had come. This made for an unpleasant, but certainly memorable, first trip to Maui for everyone on board.

The next day a series of training exercises began in earnest, the first of which was practicing beach landings. From the deck of a transport ship, Jack climbed down a rope ladder into a waiting Higgins Boat which rocked up and down in the swells of the Pacific ocean. His platoon leader, a Gunny Sergeant named Faust, began to bark a stream of orders to the men and to the Navy coxswain who was steering the vaulting vessel. To

Jack's left and right he saw what seemed like hundreds of other boats being loaded full of men and then lined up in uniform and parallel formation to the beach. As they waited in the heavy waves for every vessel to get in position, they each circled round and round in their own designated spaces. Dark clouds of smoke flowed everywhere above and between the circling crafts. One rather dimwitted young man in Jack's boat piped up with the question, "Hey Gunny, why is everyone going in circles?" Rolling his eyes impatiently at the obtuse query, the Gunny Sergeant responded sarcastically, "It's to show you how *fair* the Marine Corps is … everyone gets their share of the diesel fumes."

Within days of arrival in Maui, the men of the Fourth Division, 24th Regiment, including Private First Class Frank Jackson Matthews, had boarded the *USS Sanborn* bound for the Pacific theatre. The *Sanborn* was a Haskell-Class attack transport ship built in 1944 and a part of the Navy's Pacific fleet. She was 455 feet in length and carried a full battalion of troops and all the vehicles needed to deliver those troops onto a landing zone. She was affixed with an enormous 5"/38 mounted gun and several smaller mounted guns.

Once onboard the crowded transport ship, Jack remained confident. The men of his assigned platoon were all seasoned combat veterans having each survived several prior battles. In large part because of his comrades past success, he saw no reason to fear the upcoming engagement with the enemy. In fact, his biggest fear was that he would embarrass himself in front of the other men by doing something stupid. He wasn't precisely sure what that stupid thing might be... but he was determined that Private First Class Matthews wouldn't be the one to do it.

As had become the usual course of events for the Private, he was immediately sought out by the chaplain and pressed into service playing *Onward Christian Soldiers* on the deck of the rolling ship. When he wasn't training, or playing for the chaplain, he was composing. The *Sanborn* churned its way across the pacific seas, destination unknown, and Jack churned out notes of music into his sketch book.

On one average afternoon he stood at the ships railing, pencil and book in hand. He scribbled rhythmically as the dark cobalt water pitched itself in a fruitless attack against the steel of the ship's hull. This day, like most days, the line of men leading into the mess hall was so long that it wove in and around the deck like a heaving and impatient serpent. The railing was slippery smooth and not quite wide enough for Jack's music composition book. He had to continuously adjust and balance the small volume as he penciled down notes and tempos onto its lined white pages.

While his eyes saw the smoothly rollicking waters in front of him, his ears were shut to their sounds. In his thoughts, music notes and melodies crashed and lulled...surged, and then ebbed... climbed... and then plummeted with cacophonous resound. He shuffled a few feet forward as the serpent of men moved closer to their lunch and then once again, leaning his book on the rail, he began to scribble the sounds of music heard only in the depths of his mind.

Dear Mom and Dad,   January 1, 1945
  I arrived here (Maui) two days after Christmas. "HERE" is somewhere in the Pacific. The Fourth Marine Division captured the islands of Saipan and Tinian last summer. I'm sure we'll "hit the beach" again sooner or later. The Chaplain has a portable field organ which I am encouraged to play in my "free" time and for religious services. Today here is bright and exotic. I wonder what the new year will bring.
Love,
Jack

Six

rush - ing to join   in death

Frank Jackson Matthews
Introduction to IWO JIMA: PRELUDE

O n February 19, 1945, Jack joined his platoon in a beach landing on the shores of the tiny volcanic island of Iwo Jima. It was the afternoon of the first day of the invasion when he crowded into a tank transport ship with what seemed like a hundred other Marines.

All through the morning the smaller and more maneuverable Higgins Boats had been transporting Marines into the beach landing areas. Now, just hours later, they were full of the wounded and dying. LSM's, or *Landing Ship, Medium* as they were classified, would have to get the 24th onto the island. The LSM's were over 200 feet long and could carry five tanks and a large complement of men. Full of Marines, the LSM lurched forward and roared toward the smoking beach. From the ocean behind him Jack could see Navy ships fire their guns and land blow after blow into the interior of the island. From the sky above he heard the drone of plane engines and the whistle of bombs being freed from steel bellies. Each round of bombardment sent new streams of dark smoke into the skies. The tank ships, and Jack, were heading straight for the heart of it.

In front of the advancing LSM's lay a dark sand beach of volcanic ash just 3,500 yards long. The beach had been strategically mapped out by the Allies and divided into six color coded landing areas. Closest to the west end of the island and the looming dormant, volcanic crater of Mt. Suribachi, was Green beach. Just to the east were area's Red 1 and Red 2, followed by Yellow 1 and Yellow 2, and then finally to the far eastern side of the beach were Blue 1 and Blue 2.

The original landing site for Jack's Regiment was to be in the Blue 2 beach area. The 25th Regiment, who had gone in that morning, had taken heavy casualties there. Bodies and equipment clogged the staging area and made a beach landing anywhere near Blue completely impossible. After just a half a day's fighting only about one hundred and fifty of the nine hundred Marines assigned to the

3rd Battalion of the 25th Regiment were still alive. The surviving men desperately needed the 24th to reinforce them. Getting to the Blue area to provide the relief would take some work. Red 1, down the beach toward the West end of the island became the new target for landing. From this new landing point the men would have to hike their way into the devastated and smoldering Blue 2.

Underneath the island the Japanese had carved miles of catacombs and subterranean rooms from which they would emerge, attack, and then disappear again into safety. The 24th picked their way over the remnants of the day's earlier battles and toward their struggling brothers. As the darkness of night overtook the sky they kept to a tight formation of four-man teams by holding fast to one another's gas mask straps. This sometimes clunky configuration was made especially awkward by the dark, the smoke, the scattered debris of the first few hours of battle, and the uneven sands. The formation had its purpose. Mortars had left deep craters in the beach and when one man would slip over an edge, the others held tight to drag him back out. Jack pushed forward in clumsy unison with three other men. In the dark depths of the night, light flickered on and off from the explosion of mortars. The beams of ship spotlights were seen searching for targets. Occasionally a flare would burst overhead. For a moment the landscape would be revealed before disappearing again into the inky dark. In one of the brief flashes of light, Jack spotted an obscure figure emerging from a small hole to his immediate left. Even in the darkness of the night he could see enough of the man's uniform to identify him as a Japanese soldier. As light flashed across the man's face, Jack saw that his mouth was curled into a wry and menacing smile and his eyes were filled with a look of anticipation. The scene went dark. Then, in a split second, a random beam of light glinted off the steel of a raised Japanese sabre. Without hesitation Jack fired his weapon. Light flashed across the man once more as he collapsed next to Jack's feet. The look on his face had changed to one of total contempt. Jack wondered if the look was simple disdain for an enemy, or if the contempt was for the young Marine's unwillingness to engage the man in the elaborate swordplay that he had surely been hoping for.

Jack guessed they had lost one hundred men on the two-hour march. The dead had been left where they fell. At the end of the beach they reached the remaining men of the downtrodden and exhausted 25th and helped hold the territory that had cost so many, so much.

* * *

At daylight his platoon fought their way into the heart of the island and struggled to hold the lines across their part of the eight square miles of rocky plateaus. Jack had charged up the shifting black sand beach into the face of the enemy without hesitation or much conscious thought about what lie ahead.

His group moved steadily toward the first airfield. The ground here was open and flat. Sniper fire was coming, unseen, from somewhere in front of them. One line of Marines would run forward while another laid down a line of cover fire. Now Jack felt a wave of nearly overwhelming fear. It was hard to get up in the open and run with no cover in sight; his instinct was to stay down. He mentally willed himself to stand and run each time it was his turn to move forward. Scattered around the edges of the airfield were the remnants of wrecked planes. Sniper fire began coming from all directions. It soon became clear to the advancing platoon that the shots were coming from behind those twisted aluminum carcasses. The aircraft were providing concealment, but they couldn't provide cover. The platoon turned their machine guns on the wreckage, which proved to be no match for the Marines bullets. Soon thereafter, airfield number one was secure.

Early casualties were heavy and the carnage of the first few days was difficult to fathom, thousands had died on the first day alone. To Jack's left and his right Marines were falling victim to mortars, to sniper fire, and to the underground nets of land mines that were pre-laid by the crafty Japanese commanders. The crumpled bodies of the fallen were everywhere; on the hills, in foxholes, and even partially submerged by the tides in the dark sands of the beaches. Navy corpsman attended to the thousands of gravely wounded men as best they could. Smoldering tanks, abandoned equipment, and bloody stretchers littered the ground. Claimed territory often had to be re-claimed foot by foot by the exhausted platoons of Marines. In the greater picture, the Allied plan was working. The Japanese were pushed deeper into their tunnel system and at the same time, boxed tighter and tighter into the north side of the island. But every inch of progress was coming at a terrible cost.

On his seventh day of fighting, the nagging tooth pain that Jack had been trying to ignore since leaving Hawaii had matured to an angry crescendo. Waves of searing pain cascaded from the upper left side of his face and down through his jaw. His cheek was steadily swelling and a vague feeling of nausea was growing stronger by the minute. After returning from his morning patrol, he sat cradling his jaw in one hand and trying to will away the pain. His abject look of misery caught the eye of a passing Navy corpsman who everyone called "*Doc.*"

Doc took one look at the private's face and said matter-of-factly, "What are you sitting here for? Get down to the dentist!"

The dentist? ... Jack had never heard of such a thing. Tooth pain back home was dealt with by a pair of old pliers or not at all. In most cases one simply suffered through until the pain abated or the tooth fell out.

Doc went on to explain about this mysterious being of medical wonder known as the Navy Dentist. The corpsman assured him that he would find this strange creature seeing patients on the edge of Airfield One, now securely in Marine control. Jack was not only stunned that there existed such a person, but that he would be providing services here on this sulfur stinking, war-torn rock in the middle of the Pacific.

Aching face in one hand, he picked his way through the debris of exploded mortars and forsaken equipment, over to the side of the small airfield. Sure enough, just as the corpsman had promised, there was the man he had called the "*Dentist.*"

He was pleasant looking and wearing a somewhat tattered Navy uniform. Sitting next to him on the field was an impressive, yet puzzling, sort of contraption with pedals. The apparatus sat adjacent to a slightly reclining chair. The man quickly explained that the device of interest was a foot pump drill. Without hesitation, he hurriedly instructed the suffering private to sit down in the reclined chair and open his swollen mouth as wide as possible. The dentist mashed on the foot pedals and the machine whirred to life with a jolt. Jack instinctively braced himself for whatever was to come. The dentist worked his hands in a flurry of activity in and around the aching jaw. Above the two men the high pitched whistle of incoming Japanese mortars was heard. Cries of, "*hit the deck*," rang out all around and both men dove for cover. When the mortar had exploded, and the smoke cleared, Jack got back into the chair. The dentist once again brought the sputtering machine to life and continued his work.

Three more times Jack abandoned his chair and the dentist his pedal, to crouch down and cover themselves from the detonation of incoming mortars. At last, the infected material was removed and a filling was in its place. Jack had officially completed his first ever trip to the dentist... on the side of a bombed out airfield...on Iwo Jima.

He got up from the chair and made his way back to his platoon. In that moment he never would have dreamed that the filling completed so hurriedly, and under the screams of incoming mortars, would be with him as solid as the day it was placed for decades to come.

* * *

One day while on patrol, a flamethrower opera-
tor near Jack was picked off by an enemy sniper.
Almost before the cumbersome weapon hit the ground,
the Gunny Sergeant had yelled for Jack to put it on.
Being more scared of the Gunny Sergeant than he was
of the Japanese, Jack hurriedly strapped on the three
heavy tanks of fuel and compressed gas.

Private Barowski, A big Polish lumberjack from
Washington State, yelled from the other side of the fall-
en Marines body, "Hey Gunny...give me that thrower,
Matthews is just a skinny kid from South Carolina."

"I'll tell you Ski," hollered back the Gunny, "I'm not
so much looking for a strong back and weak mind."

Jack understood the Gunny's reasoning. The flamethrower seemed like a brutish weapon but it took smarts
to use it to the platoon's advantage. Jack realized that
you had to know where everyone in your group was before you pulled the trigger or you could easily inciner-
ate your own men. The deadly nozzle of the thrower
spewed choking gas and flames. Small and strategic
bursts at the right time and the right place were critical calculations. A single tank of fuel, that might carry
just a few minutes worth of flame, sometimes had to last
you all day. From that point on, for day after day, he
marched up and down the island on patrols carrying
the eighty pound tanks on his back. He worked quickly from tunnel to tunnel, chasing the enemy into the

darkness, burning out their hideaways, and then using the gruesome power of his weapon to suck out all the life-giving oxygen from their cave system. Frequently he would clear a tunnel one day only to find it filled with the enemy again the very next.

The Japanese were relentless in their attacks. He seldom saw the faces of the men; they were mere shadows in the mouths of caves. But he knew…*he knew*… that the shadows were human beings. They were human beings that he was burning…and he *hated* it. He felt disgust at what had to be done, and a sense of rebellion and resentment toward the weapon he carried. The options were to kill or be killed…to kill or watch a fellow Marine be killed. So, day after day, he pushed forward, firing the flamethrower and clearing the labyrinth of underground tunnels of its enemy occupants.

If the days were bad, *and they were*, then the nights were mostly worse. On a good night he sought solace in a foxhole he had dug out of the acrid volcanic ash and soil. He found a few bloody and discarded gurneys that provided a makeshift roof from the frequent rains and willed himself to rest. Often the night would simply mean more patrols. In many ways the night was more dangerous for the men because it was under cover of dark that the Japs would emerge from their hiding places and pill boxes and attempt to infiltrate back into the Marine's territory.

Patrols passing in the dark through checkpoints had a system for sorting out friendly troops from the enemy trying to perform a sneak attack. It was a simple password system that would vary on a nightly basis.

On one particular night the password was the name of any American President. It was something all Marines would have an instant answer to, but the typical Japanese grunt would struggle with. While the system was simplistic, it was also a deadly serious protective measure for the Marines.

At each checkpoint a voice unseen from the dark would ask, "What's the password?"

In response to the query a patrol member would quickly name an American president or risk being immediately dispatched by rifle fire. After the recognized president was named then the voice from the dark would confirm his own friendly identity by also naming any president in return. Then the patrol would continue on its way until the process played itself out again at the next checkpoint.

As they proceeded creeping through the darkness, Jack would periodically hear a Marine give the password, "Washington."

To which a faceless voice would respond, "Roosevelt."

Frequently he would hear the name, "Lincoln."

Once a responder was even heard to name, "Jefferson"… and on the patrol went.

One young private in the group that evening was, "*the Professor*"; so named because he had a year of Harvard education under his belt and made certain everyone knew it. The Professor liked nothing better than to boast about his intellectual prowess. Jack and the other privates considered him to be a big-headed braggart and generally *stuck up as all hell*. The Professor happened to be the lead man that night as the group passed one particular checkpoint. Out of the dark, a slow, thick Mississippi accent filled the night air with the stern query, "What's the password?"

To which the Professor haughtily responded, "Tyler."

Dead silence followed for several seconds and then the same slow voice was heard asking, "Hey Charlie, was Tyler a president?" ...followed by the distinct clicking sound of a round being centered in a rifle.

Frantic whispers of, "Oh crap!" could be heard as Jack's platoon hit the ground and the Professor -with gun held up in both hands over his head- yelled, "Jesus Christ don't shoot!" Followed immediately by a tumbling and rapid-fire recitation of: "WashingtonAdamsJeffersonMadisonMonroeAdamsJacksonVanBurenHarrison........."

He got all the way to "Lincoln" before the patrol, unsuccessful at stifling their laughter any longer, drowned out the sound of his panic-stricken voice. In the darkness of Iwo Jima the Professor had finally been schooled.

* * *

Moments of levity were rare and brief on the stinking island. Death was overwhelming and everywhere.

Because of the Japanese method of using tunnels and hideaways there was no front line... *no truly secured zone...* and no area of respite. An area cleared of Japanese one hour might be filled with machine gun fire and exploding grenades the very next. There was never a moment in any hour, day or night, that Jack and every other Marine were not acutely aware that these minutes might be their last.

On one clear afternoon Jack's patrol group crept their way in a loose formation in and out of the rock strewn and hillocky fields around airfield number one. As they hiked, Jack recalled vividly the briefing his group had received aboard ship about the significance of Iwo Jima to the Allied efforts.

The strategic importance of the minuscule volcanic island was as a fueling stop for American planes. The island, with its three airfields, sat between American held airfields in the Mariana Islands and the Japanese mainland. American bombers stationed in the string of US-held islands had to carry enough fuel to take them all the way from the Mariana's to the Japanese

Mainland and back. Carrying so much fuel onboard meant less cargo weight could be allocated to carrying bombs. Furthermore, because of the distance involved, the bombers had to travel unaccompanied and thus unprotected by American fighter planes. The smaller and faster fighters simply could not carry enough fuel onboard to make the round trip. This left the aircraft, its pay load of explosives, and its crew, vulnerable to attack by Japanese fighter planes. Any planes that were shot up by the enemy had little chance of limping all the way back to the Marianna Islands. By securing the airfields of Iwo Jima, the United States would possess both a valuable fueling station and a landing zone for damaged planes.

The capture of Iwo Jima was not only of strategic offensive importance, but defensive importance as well. The Japanese were using the island's central location to spot incoming Allied forces. Lookouts would dispatch warnings to the mainland, thus allowing the Japanese ample time to prepare their defenses. And if those weren't enough reasons to capture and control the island, there was another sobering reality. When the time eventually came for an attack on mainland Japan, the island would serve as an Allied base and jumping-off point for the massive invasion.

The radio Jack's patrol carried suddenly crackled and leapt to life with an incoming message for the

Gunny. From his position Jack strained to hear what the message was. The voice on the other end of the transmission had a special assignment for the men. An American B29 plane was heading toward the airfield and it was coming in fast with extensive damage from enemy fire, and almost no fuel. The pilot was not sure he would make it there at all. If by some miracle he did arrive, then the patrols instructions were to provide him and the plane with cover and get him to safety.

Gunny gave the orders for the men's positions and then called over one of Jack's patrol mates, affectionately known as, "*Rooster*," for a special assignment. Rooster was a hyperactive young marine with freckled fair skin and a distinct amount of country naiveté. His avian nickname certainly fit his personality, but the apt moniker was actually inspired by the shock of rooster red hair on the top of his head. Gunny told Rooster to hightail it down onto the open airfield and, if the pilot made it, he was to tell him that the airfield was securely under Marine control.

Rooster double-timed it down to the field, his helmeted head disappearing through the folds of rock and ash. Within a few minutes the roaring and sputtering of the B29 could be heard echoing off the rocks from all around the patrol's positions. The engines groaned and shuddered like a great dying beast and the plane seemed to alternately lurch and then hesitate in the air. The sides of the craft were riddled with gunfire and thick dark smoke curled from under its belly.

Miraculously the pilot brought the craft down in one piece onto the landing strip. A brief cheer rippled through the patrol and soon two figures, presumably that of Rooster and the pilot, could be seen as blurry moving forms in the distance. Rooster, who was breathless and clearly distraught, ran to meet the group. The Gunny took him by the shoulders and gave him a quick shake, "Rooster" he said, "what in the world is the matter with you, the plane made it."

"I know Gunny," stammered the shaken Rooster, his freckles now hidden by the bright red flush of his face; "But, you won't believe what that pilot done! … He got out of the plane, kneeled down, and kissed the ground… Then he got up, grabbed me… took my helmet off… and kissed the top of my head! …and him a decorated Captain and me a Lance Corporal!"

Gunny belly-laughed aloud and replied, "Well Rooster, just be glad you wasn't a Sergeant or he would've kissed you on the lips!"

Seven

Trou - ble, Old Man Trou - ble done found me.

Frank Jackson Matthews
Here Comes Satchmo

As the days went on, the Japanese clung desperately to their remaining territory and fought to the bitter death at every turn. Each day Jack lost more and more platoon members. Some fell to sniper fire, others to mortar attacks, and many to the exploding mines that the Japanese had sprinkled throughout the hot, stinking soil.

For Jack and the others there was no time to process the losses, no time to consciously digest the horror around them. Like his fellow Marines, he had to simply press forward, complete his patrols, and perform his duties. There weren't many breaks other than those necessary to answer the call of nature, or eat a few rations. Jack didn't mind the pre-packaged rations so much. Sure the small tin of unidentifiable meat product was not the greatest; but each cardboard box also contained four cigarettes, and a chocolate bar. Since he didn't smoke, he was always able to trade off his tobacco for more chocolate.

Each night Jack was amazed that his slight one hundred and fifty pound frame made it back to a foxhole in the ground. By now he had been wounded three times. Once a large shard of metal had shot into his skull just above his left eye and just below where his helmet provided protection. Not wanting to be sent out to a hospital ship, he talked a medic into pulling it out with a pair of pliers. A few days later, an explosion knocked him to the ground wrenching his back and bruising his spine. The men next to him weren't so lucky. Then he took a Japanese grenade to the arm and wrist. Ceramic shrapnel tore through his flesh and lodged deep into and around his tendons and veins.

By this time in the war the Japanese had depleted their supply of raw materials and had resorted to creating grenades from ceramics. Japanese kilns that had once produced fine pottery now wrought glazed orbs of terra cotta prized not for their beauty, but for their ability to kill American troops. There was no time to attempt removal of the ceramic shards that had ripped and seared into his muscle and tissue. A Navy corpsman hurriedly tacked back together and bandaged what was left of the skin.

As he tramped up and down the island he pushed out all thoughts of anything but his task. To dwell on the fact that a Marine with a flamethrower was an easy target for the snipers would have been pointless and distracting. Distraction could have meant death.

A new patrol assignment came through and Jack found himself hiking deep into the north side of the island. A large network of caves had been blown open and exposed by a Battle Ship and Jack's patrol group was sent in to ensure that the Japanese were gone and their weapons destroyed. The main cave was now more of a gaping hole in the rock foundation of the island. It contained what was left of the largest mounted gun that Jack had seen since arriving on land. The gun fired sixteen-inch mortars and the Japanese had undoubtedly used the behemoth to target planes, tanks, and anything else they could sight. They surely had done some damage with this weapon, but their massive firepower had ultimately given away their underground position. Now the roof of the cave was laid open like the peeled back lid of a tin can and the gun was twisted and blackened past all recognition.

Branching off of what was formerly the main cave were numerous large tunnels. These tunnels were larger and wider than others Jack had encountered, but not much brighter, and just as dangerous. He gripped tightly to the flamethrower and walked slowly into what appeared to be a central passage. The cave was dry and dark and the pungent smell of sweat mingled with the unrelenting scents of gunpowder, kerosene, and the ever-present choking sulfur. Jack wasn't sure if the odor was the stench of the cave or if he smelled his own stinking gear. His eyes strained to adjust to what little light was available. He could see large crates scattered about here and there, some were stacked neatly, but most were jumbled or broken in heaps. A few ripped Japanese uniforms lay strewn about with what looked like empty food tins and a handful of dented canteens. This, he thought, was obviously a living quarters for the Japs manning the big gun.

He stepped cautiously forward and quickly scanned the walls of the cave to the left and the right. He listened intently for even the smallest sound or indication that it might still be occupied by even one lone Japanese soldier. There was nothing but silence. The Japanese forces had proven to be a fearless and unswerving enemy, but one that was now devastated by the relentless American forces. Still, there was no room for error. He took another guarded step forward and through the sole of his boot felt a slight change in the texture of the cave floor. He risked a momentary glance down and saw that a number of square cards dotted the ground. Without taking his eyes off of the tunnel in front of him, or his finger off the trigger of the flamethrower, he bent at the knees and hastily picked up a handful of the slick cards. Glancing quickly, he saw they were some kind of playing cards. "*Those bastards*," thought Jack, "*they were up here playing poker and picking us off with that damn gun.*" The flash of righteous anger he had indulged in suddenly turned to surprise and amusement as he flipped the cards in his hand over.

Depicted on the reverse side of each one, in full color, were large breasted Japanese women in various stages of undress. They were placed in different scenes, sporting different hairstyles, and various outfits…or *no outfits* at all. The one thing they all had in common were cartoonishly large breasts. The young marine almost couldn't believe what he was seeing. Not that he was a stranger to the attributes of the fairer sex. Pin-ups girls were all the rage both in basic training and aboard ship. But this…this was something altogether different. Of all the things he had seen in combat this was, without a doubt, the most unexpected.

Even as a subconscious flush of color crept into Jack's cheeks his practical mind began to overtake his initial feelings of astonishment. Making a quick mental calculation he figured each card could sell for five dollars to the boys on the return ship. The *return* ship…this was the first time he had allowed himself to consider that there might be a return ship for him…the first time he had thought in concrete terms that there might be a future beyond this island.

Until now he had just pushed forward, living only in the moments between each explosion, in the time between each step of a patrol, in one drink from a canteen, in a single laugh, in a single moment's rest. Did he actually believe he would leave this place alive? Did he believe he had a future longer than the next fleeting moment…? He did.

The thought was both exhilarating and frightening. The rats had been chased out of their holes, their caves were blown to pieces, and their guns would fire no more. For the first time since that dark march on the beach, he had the indelible feeling that the largest hill had been climbed. Somehow, through each sacrifice and each act of courage, they had reached the summit and were clutching victory tightly as they ran down the other side. He hurriedly snatched up a few handfuls of the cards from the cave floor and stuffed them deep into his trouser pockets. Turning out of the tunnels and back toward the open he took with him more than his pocketful of salacious commodity, he took the realization that for him a life beyond this island was still ahead.

* * *

It was now March 17, 1945 and the eighteen-year-old private had been in combat on Iwo Jima for nearly a month. The Marines had essentially conquered the entire island, save for a few straggling Japanese soldiers still hiding in the underground tunnels. The airfields were secure and due to be turned over to the command of the Air Force. The landing beaches, Mount Suribachi, and the rocky blood soaked hillocks in-between were all inextricably in Allied hands.

Jack sat resting on the ground with his returning patrol group. His wrist was aching more than usual today and he rubbed the dirty bandage that encircled it and held together his tattered flesh. By now he was the last surviving member of his original forty-man platoon. From somewhere among the numbers of resting Marines he heard a voice calling:

"Matthews... Matthews... has anyone seen Matthews?"

"He's over here," an anonymous voice directed.

Jack looked up to see a familiar face approaching - it was the 4th Division chaplain.

"I've been looking all over for you Matthews," the chaplain's friendly voice boomed, "I want to have some services for the men tomorrow and I need you to play the organ."

In disbelief Jack stammered, "You have an organ with you? ... Here?"

"Well yes," chuckled the chaplain, "my little reed organ."

Jack was familiar with the instrument. The small packable organ would be similar to the ones he had played for his father's revivals back home.

The chaplain grinned at him, "I only brought it with me because I knew you would be here to play it."

Jack's mind flashed back over the last month. His minister father would have called it nothing short of a miracle that he was standing here talking with the chaplain and not lying lifeless under the fields of white crosses nearby.

His mind snapped back to the present, to the chaplain standing in front of him, and to his odd request for an organist. All he could think to ask was, "What do you want me to play?"

"Just pick two hymns. We'll alternate Protestant and Catholic services so pick something that they will all know, but nothing they have to sing." The chaplain's face changed and his normally broad smile tightened down as he added, "They'll be too tired to sing." He took a breath and his face eased again into its characteristic grin. "And of course," he continued, "You'll need to play the National Anthem."

As he walked away he turned and added in a cautionary tone: "But Matthews… play a version that has some life to it… so they can stand proud."

That night Jack got busy arranging in his mind a spirited version of the National Anthem and he thought hard about what two hymns should be played. He decided on, *Jesu, Joy of Man's Desiring,* as it would be easily recognized by both the Catholics and the Protestants and didn't require any singing by the tired men. For the second hymn he selected, *My Faith Looks Up To Thee,* the song's fourth stanza seemed to speak to what he knew was on the minds of his fellow Marines, what was on his mind… all those who were no longer with them. All those white crosses.

> *When ends life's transient dream,*
> *When death's cold, sullen stream shall o'er me roll;*
> *Blest Savior, then in love, fear and distrust remove;*
> *O bear me safe above, a ransomed, soul!*

Early Sunday morning Jack unfolded the suitcase sized organ as the first group of men gathered around. The fatigued men sat on crates, on boxes, on the ground. They listened to the chaplain and they bowed their heads in prayer. Jack peddled hard on the organ and got as much volume as he could from the diminutive instrument. A few of the men quietly sang along, but most sat silent and stone faced, exhausted, simply drinking in every bit of comfort that the music could provide. When he played his arrangement of the National Anthem everyone stood tall, even as tears filled some of their eyes. The groups of men kept coming all day long, twenty or thirty at a time, seeking a few moments of reflection and consolation. His bandaged wrist throbbed as he pounded on the keys of the organ. Men kept coming to share in the reassurance of the services. He counted out ten services, and then twenty, then he lost count. For as long as the men kept coming, Jack kept playing.

When the services were done for the day he walked to the makeshift cemetery and wandered alone among the rows of white crosses. The remains of his platoon lay under his feet and his arrangement of the National Anthem rang in his ears. The next day he left the island on a ship bound for Hawaii.

Eight

I am filled with nau - sea and con-tempt!

Frank Jackson Matthews
Introduction to Iwo Jima: Passacaglia

T he ship that provided passage back to Hawaii for
Jack and some of his fellow Marines was the *USS
President Polk*. The *Polk* had been born in the shipyards
of Virginia as a luxury cruise liner. It was one of a number of cruise ships that were conscripted for use by the
Navy, and then transformed into ships of war that could
carry cargo, troops, or both.

Off the shores of Iwo Jima, he climbed his way
up the *Polk's* sixty foot cargo net. The ship bore no

resemblance to the luxury liners that he had seen photos of in the library back home. Rather than wide staircases and tastefully appointed suites, there were a series of utilitarian metal ladders. At the end of the ladders were bunks made of aluminum piping and canvas that climbed up twelve levels. For those on the top bunk it was a slow and careful ascent past eleven other sleeping Marines. Instead of catering to waltzing starlets, the *Polk* was earning battle stars.

As he made his way back across the Pacific, Jack's thoughts were consumed with all he had experienced on Iwo Jima. The knowledge of what he had accomplished, and the astonishing fact that he was alive, banged in discordance against the jarring sounds of plane engines and exploding mortars. The smell of the flamethrower lingered on his clothes and in the pores of his skin. Memories bubbled and swirled through his mind; …the faces of friends…the gnarled face of a dead Japanese soldier…a blood filled helmet… the shadows.

He was filled with anger. He was angry at the loss of so much young life. He was angry at the now piteous enemy. He was angry at what he had been forced to do and to see. To deal with this avalanche of thoughts and feelings Jack turned to what he knew best and began to write music.

In his mind he heard the contemplative and maudlin notes of the oboe. The strains of the oboe morphed into the ominous dark power of the French horn as it foretold danger and rancorous dark ruin. He heard the deep plaintive sounds of the bassoon. Within its low timbres he could almost discern the grim mourning of a man. This, he felt, was the saddest instrument of all.

The compositions could have easily been a mass of tangled and violent crescendos reflecting his deep fury and profound sadness over the tragedies of the last month. It was only the presence of a more natural and quiet sorrow that tempered his writing. Back in December, while Jack had been headed for Maui, word had come that one of his musical heroes, the great Glenn Miller, had died in Europe. At the time, all focus had been on his role as *Frank, the Private First Class,* and there had been no opportunity for *Jack, the Composer,* to mourn this loss. Now he pulled from that sadness. It allowed into his music the rich harmonies and distinctive sax settings that he so admired in Miller's playing.

The notes and scores poured forth easily. Using the talent that God had given him, he wrote away the horror and turned it into something new and fresh, something ... *alive.* The time spent composing was both productive and cathartic. As the engines of the transport ship churned their way toward Hawaii, Jack's mind turned over each of his feelings and memories into a symphony performance of all he had experienced on that bloody, stinking rock in the Pacific.

After a time the writing began to take on some aspects of reconciliation and happiness. He was happy to be returning to Maui. Heck, he was happy to be returning to *anywhere*...but especially Maui. It was a place whose warm sun, cool breezes, and divine flora resonated with him. He finished writing about Iwo and began writing a piece about the islands in the style of Duke Ellington. Ellington was a pianist like Jack and tended to write music in a style that was direct, logical, and uncluttered. Jack admired those characteristics, and after the chaos of Iwo it was what his mind needed. He wanted to think about simple things, things that made sense, beautiful things. When the composition was finished he named it, *Anthurium*, after one of the beautiful Hawaiian flowers he had seen on Maui.

Not that all his time shipboard was spent in such a noble pursuits as music composition. Meal time provided a distraction to all the men on the journey home and it was a time that Jack normally spent talking about news of war or swapping jokes with his fellow survivors of that dark island.

In the ship's galley, a crew of Navy cooks would serve three meals a day for Jack and his fellow Marines. The menu was rudimentary and prepared without any finesse. If Jack was lucky, the hot food would be hot, and the cold food cold, and that was about as much as he could hope for. A typical meal was a serving of Spam and some reconstituted potatoes.

The lack of appetizing food was made worse by the fact that it was always being served by a couple of the dirtiest, rough-looking mess-hall cooks that Jack had ever set eyes on. Their faces, which were covered in stubble and sweat, appropriately complimented their saggy yellowing tee-shirts which were stained with splatters of grease, and the distinct outlines of filthy handprints.

One day at lunch Jack sat stirring his potatoes in bored contemplation and studying the back of the galley serving line. Behind the line, covering the breadth of the entire wall was a life-size and full-color paper mural. On the mural were pictured two clean cut and spotlessly uniformed sailors. Trim, healthy looking, and with big solicitous smiles on their faces, the men depicted were the picture of Navy pride. The food they were serving was fresh, of diverse variety, and appeared exceptionally appetizing. Spelled out on the top of the scene in giant black lettering were the words:

"Food Will Win the War."

The contrast between the optimism of the mural and the reality of the dismal chow line was striking. Jack could not help but be amused, and a little irritated, at the irony before him.

That afternoon he quietly secured a red grease pen and gathered together a few of his fellow privates to assist him. The band of young men waited patiently until the lull between the lunch and dinner meals when the galley emptied out and the cooks were busily distracted in the kitchen. Silently, Jack's recruits formed a human screen between the dining hall and the passage in an effort to obscure the view of any officer who just might be passing by. Jack crept into the dim, empty galley, grease pen in hand.

He climbed up on the nearest stool, and below the Navy proclamation of: "Food Will Win the War," he boldly wrote in large red letters, "Yes, but how do we get the enemy to eat it?"

Nine

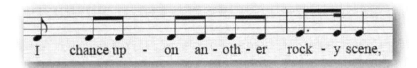

I chance up - on an - oth - er rock - y scene,

Frank Jackson Matthews
Introduction to Iwo Jima: Passacaglia

Jack's new home for the near future was the Fourth Division Marine Camp on the Hawaiian island of Maui. Practically named, "*Camp Maui*," it was situated in a barren area at the base of the dormant volcano, Haleakala.

Initially the camp wasn't much more than a rudimentary set-up consisting of rows of canvas tents, a mess hall, and some hastily built offices. He shared his tent with several other Marines and a large supply of mud that was produced on a regular basis by the heavy afternoon rains. He washed his clothes in a bucket of water and hung them to dry in the hot morning sun; he pressed them by laying them flat under the thin mattress of his cot and sleeping on them at night. Training exercises continued on a daily basis and included hiking up the slopes of the volcanic crater, drills in the Hawaiian jungles, and of course taking care of his equipment, the still stinking, and still heavy, flamethrower.

For the first time in his marine training something new was added; house to house fighting tactics. Soon thereafter, a set of winter clothing was issued to each man. These additions did not take an Einstein to figure out; it all indicated that the next target would be mainland Japan.

By his nineteenth birthday in June, Jack had received a promotion to corporal. In the eyes of the arriving Marines he was an old man, a survivor of Iwo, and a seasoned combat veteran. He would have thought it all to be very heady stuff had it not been for the scuttlebutt around camp that their expected casualties in Japan were going to be 95%.

In their tents, Jack and the other Marines figured up their service points. The Marines worked on a points system where each man earned credits for things like time served, battle experience, and even marital status. According to the current point scale Jack was still nowhere close to being sent home, so he continued with the daily routine of drills, training, and life in Camp Maui.

The camp was developing at a steady pace. There were some sports fields, an outdoor movie area, and a makeshift chapel. Off of the base there wasn't much to do that Jack could afford. Some of the guys would go into the nearby towns for drinks and dancing, but all of Jack's pay was going into war bonds. The pressure on young Marines to buy bonds from each pay was significant. Some resisted the pressure and saved their pay for free time and recreational pursuits. Jack knew that when he got back home every dollar from those bonds would be needed to pay for an education.

His one luxury expenditure was a five-cent bottle of Coke that he would buy in the camp store. Each day following lunch in the mess hall, Jack would trade in a nickel for a glass bottle of the fizzy refreshment. He would carry his prize over to the base of a nearby tree to sit in the shade and drink it covetously while dreaming of the day he would be home and away from that putrid flamethrower.

At the same time that Jack was bemoaning his seemingly inexorable tie to that dismal weapon, divine intervention was taking place in the form of a General's desire for diversion.

General Clifton Bledsoe Cates, the 4th Division commander, was born in Tiptonville, Tennessee, and had earned his stars serving in France during the First World

War. Cates was a hero of the infamous battle of Belleau Wood.

Belleau Wood was an area of France near the Marne River that Cates helped his fellow Marines successfully defend from the Germans in 1918. While the French soldiers repeatedly retreated, their allies, the American Marines, remained determined to root out the Germans from the heavily forested area. Having run out of ammunition, the Marines used bayonets and their fists to win the battle. In its time, Belleau Wood represented the largest battle, and the largest number of losses, in the history of the Marine Corps. It was also considered to be their greatest demonstration of heroism. The Battle's infamy was finally eclipsed by the Battle of Iwo Jima.

The hero and division commander now wanted to establish an officer's club for Camp Maui. The general rented a building near the base which he ordered to be fixed up and fashioned into a piano bar. When he asked the chaplain who could play the club's newly acquired piano, the answer was: "The only guy I know is that little corporal Matthews."

Overnight, Jack's primary duties were transferred from the flamethrower to the service of the division headquarters. During the days he would continue with routine Marine training exercises, and at night he would play for the pleasure of the officers. Jack made sure to play with an emphasis on old French standards that he knew would appeal to the general. It was a savvy move that got Cates' attention and favor. The general quickly decided to put the corporal's talent for entertainment to use in the realm of diplomacy.

The local populations of native Hawaiian people were steadily and enthusiastically warming to the presence of Marines on their island home. With the attack on Pearl Harbor and the ensuing war, the worlds of American military operations and Hawaiian village life had collided. While Hawaiians embraced and even celebrated the Marines 4th division as their own, there were still aspects of native Hawaiian life that were kept separate. Troops did not generally go into indigenous village areas. Both the Marines and the natives of Maui worked at forging continued appreciation of one another. One of General Cates' ideas in this regard was to have Jack attend the local's Sunday church services. Turned out in his best dress khakis, he would play piano for them as a gesture of goodwill.

The island was dotted with a number of Congregationalist Christian churches. In the history of seventeenth century Hawaii, the arrival of Protestant Congregationalist missionaries had played a key role in shaping the current religious beliefs and traditions of the native people. The church missionaries arrived in 1820 and began work in setting up schools, establishing a written version of the Hawaiian language, and introducing the natives to a Christian God. Over the next several years more and more Congregationalist missionaries sailed to Hawaii with the goal of building schools, establishing churches, and providing medical care to the indigenous people.

On Maui, the Reverend Dwight Baldwin had established himself as a central figure in the medical and spiritual care of the Hawaiian people. His work to educate and care for the island helped prosper the Congregationalist religion. By the early 1900's a number of Christian churches were thriving.

Jack was well educated on this era of Maui's religious history and was versed in the assemblage's traditional hymns. He had a natural advantage to acceptance through his parent's Congregationalist past. When the Hawaiians would ultimately learn that both of his parents were graduates of a Congregationalist seminary, Jack felt certain he would be accepted wholeheartedly by otherwise potentially skeptical natives.

Before Corporal Matthews could wow the natives with his heritage and piano playing, he would first have to get from the Marine Camp to the church. Unfortunately, the nineteen-year-old corporal couldn't drive.

When he had left South Carolina, car fuel had been strictly rationed and rubber was scarce. Jack, along with many other teenage boys, could not use the community's meager resources for superfluous things like driving lessons or Saturday night dates. So, while he could be called a seasoned combat veteran, Jack had no idea on earth how to drive a jeep from one end of Maui to the other. General Cates had an easy solution for this problem; he would simply have one of the young officers of Camp Maui drive Jack to the village.

For the task at hand the general selected the serious and accomplished First Lieutenant Willis. Willis, an attractive and ambitious young man, was ordered to gas-up a jeep, dress in his officers clothes, and act as chauffeur for the young corporal pianist. In the general's estimation it was wholly appropriate for an entry level officer to be part of this important local diplomatic mission. Unfortunately, First Lieutenant Willis did not exactly agree.

To the lieutenant it was an utter insult that he, as an officer, would be serving as a mere shuttle driver to this skinny young corporal. Willis's attitude about the assignment was not helped by the immediate and unrelenting ribbings he began taking from the other officers.

On that first Sunday excursion, having been mercilessly mocked by his peers, Lieutenant Willis climbed in the driver's seat of the jeep with a scowl on his face and the attitude of an agitated yellow jacket. The two

Marines rode along at a brisk pace in marked heavy silence until the jeep came to a sudden jolting halt in front of a pretty, white clapboard church with a small cross sitting prominently at the top of its wide central spire.

The service went exceedingly well. After Jack's successful performance they were heartily invited outside to attend the luau style celebration that took place after each Sunday service. The grounds of the church were lush and tropical. The foods were plentiful and sumptuous. Even more plentiful and sumptuous were the beautiful native island girls that doted on the two young Marines. Jack noted that on the trip home the lieutenant's attitude was much improved to say the least. However, still stinging from the mocking he received from his fellow officers, Willis made the naïve mistake of bragging to them about his plum assignment. By the following week there was a waiting list of over one hundred officers volunteering to be the driver for Corporal Matthews. To Jack's surprise the list to be his Sunday chauffeur included all the minor officers, several colonels, and even a two-star general. After seeing the list, General Cates was forced to issue a statement noting that it would be "*inappropriate*" for an officer higher than captain to place his name on the "*chauffeuring Matthews*" list.

Dear Mom and Dad,   June 12, 1945
   Last Sunday the Chaplain "volunteered" me to play the organ at a lovely local church. I didn't have any music so I sorta composed something. I'm afraid the music was rather sad since we are all depressed from the battle of Iwo Jima. However, we are already getting ready for the "next one".
Love,
Jack

P.S. Last week on my 19th birthday, I was promoted to Corporal!

* * *

On August fifteenth, 1945, word came to Camp Maui of the Japanese surrender. Celebration was in order and well earned by the men of the Fourth.

   The commanders knew that all the men in camp, officers and enlisted alike, would be drunk by the end of the night. It was common knowledge that Corporal Jack Matthews didn't drink at all; he simply didn't like the taste of beer and never had. Someone had to remain clearheaded. So, Jack was selected to be the *sole* sober man on duty.

The festivities commenced with music, toasting, and general merriment. Soon the sound of celebratory gunfire could be heard across the camp. Glasses were raised to fallen brethren, to the Marine Corps, to victory, and to the prospects of going home.

Some of the local children that would frequent the base were enjoying the revelry of the moment as well. It was common to see children, especially those who were partially of Japanese heritage, hanging around the 4th Division. Many of them were from families taken to the Japanese Internment camp which was situated very near the Marine encampment in an area called Haiku. The youngsters would hang around and entertain themselves by watching the Marine's activities and to plead for candy and other trinkets that the young men might have handy.

On this festive night the little scamps celebrated the end of the war with their military neighbors. Some of them received a double dose of the Marine's generosity as treats were given with abandon in the spirit of the occasion. One young boy of about ten years of age was horse-playing with several friends and a group of laughing and intoxicated Marines. In light of the celebration, guns were loaded only with blanks.

In broken English the boy gleefully begged one of the men to shoot him and pulled the gun over and over into the center of his tummy. Influenced by foggy judgment, and not believing there was any harm in indulging the young urchin, the Marine fired the blank. The wadding struck the boys tender abdomen and he crumpled to the ground.

When Jack arrived on the chaotic and confused scene the boy was pale, listless, and blood was gushing from his small mouth. The camp medics were all soused beyond the ability to respond in any meaningful way. Jack called for the chaplain, less for spiritual assistance and more because he was the only reasonably sober soul in the camp.

Together they raced to do what they could for the child and finally managed to contact a local hospital for help. It was either too late, or maybe there had never been a chance at all. The boy was lifeless.

Jack returned to his duty station and in silence began to complete the necessary reports. He had done everything that a sober corporal could be expected to do in the situation. There was nothing left for him to feel bad about.

Dear Mom and Dad,   August, 1945
    Hallelujah! War is over! And just in time too: We were issued winter clothing last month, which probably means

Japan would have been our next operation. Now, they're actually letting us get out and enjoy Maui a little. The flowers here are quite beautiful and the music in my head is very "South Sea", or maybe I've been watching too many Dorothy Lamour movies.
Love,
Jack

Jack at age fifteen with parents Curtis and Mary Matthews, and sister June, in Newberry, South Carolina

Portrait of piano teacher and composer, Mrs. Crosby
Adams, (Born Juliette Aurelia Graves). Photo Courtesy
of Presbyterian Heritage Center, Montreat.

The *House in the Woods* at Montreat. This was the residence of
Mr. and Mrs. Crosby Adams where Jack received summer piano
lessons. Here he learned the value of composing music in his
mind without the assistance of a piano and was inspired to teach
music. Photo Courtesy of Presbyterian Heritage Center, Montreat.

Ships and equipment litter the beaches of Iwo Jima after being shelled by the Japanese or bogged down in the island's black sands. Mt. Suribachi can be seen looming in the background. Photo courtesy of the National Archives.

5th Division Marines inch up Red Beach 1. Many Marines never made it past the beach. Photo courtesy of the National Archives.

4th Division Marines shell enemy positions,
mostly hidden in caves and tunnels on Iwo Jima.
Photo Courtesy of the National Archives.

The world famous photo of the American flag being raised
on Mount Suribachi. The photo was taken on February 23,
1945 just five days into the fighting. The iconic photo has
become a symbol of the Marine Corps and American tenacity.
Photo by Joe Rosenthal courtesy of the National Archive.

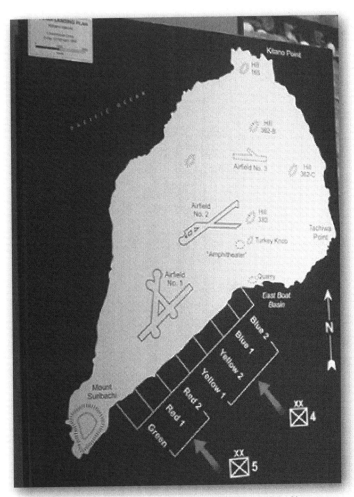

Map of Iwo Jima illustrating the various landing beaches, the airfields, and Mount Suribachi at the far southern tip of the island. Photo courtesy of the National Museum of the Marine Corps.

At age eighteen, Frank Jackson Matthews was a combat tested Marine with the Fourth Division. This official Marine Corps photo was taken at "Camp Maui" in 1945; about two months after the battle of Iwo Jima had ended.

Jack plays piano in the student center at the University of North Carolina at Chapel Hill. He was the official pianist and musical director for the University's acclaimed performance group, *The Sound and Fury.*

Taken at Quantico in 1951, this official Marine Corps photo shows the newly minted officer, Frank Jackson Matthews.

The distinctive spires and coastline of the historic Hotel del Coronado. "The Del", was built in 1888 in an astonishing eleven short months through the use of its own on-site manufacturing of the materials needed for construction. Photo courtesy of the Hotel del Coronado.

Matthews (standing right) answers questions from a visiting General while serving in the Army as a Captain and the Enlisted Detachment Commander at Fort Polk, Louisiana. Not only was Jack in the Marine Corps and the Army, but he also had a short period of service in the Air Force as an aviation cadet during an exchange opportunity. He decided fairly quickly that he was a Marine at heart and received an honorable discharge from the Air Force and re-entered the Marine Corps.

Playing the piano in the living room of his first home
as a married man in Baton Rouge, Louisiana.

Jack is shown, seated to the right, in this advertisement for
the "Date on 28" television show, a daily variety show in Baton
Rouge, Louisiana, for which he played a Hammond organ.

Jack with his beautiful Margaret. Enjoying dinner
at Caesar's Palace restaurant in Lake Tahoe.

The National Museum of the Marine Corps tells the
story of the Corps from its beginnings in Tun Tavern in
1775 to modern day operations around the world.

Being able to share memories of the past with other World War II veterans is one of Jack's favorite and most important roles as a docent.

Jack swaps stories with a visiting Marine Corps Veteran.
Here he discusses the finer points of the flamethrower
as a weapon. Heavy and highly effective, it was key for
routing the enemy out of the miles of subterranean caves
and tunnels carved throughout the island of Iwo Jima.

Jack's daughter Janet, and nephew Mike, study the tanks of a flamethrower on display at the National Museum of the Marine Corps. The weapon is identical to the one carried by Marines on Iwo Jima.

Always animated, Jack tells a story about landing on Red Beach on Iwo Jima, February 19th, 1945.

Matthews stands in front of the very flag that he watched lowered from the summit of Mt. Suribachi on Iwo Jima over 70 years ago.

Helping to inspire a new generation of Marines, the Marine Corp's Frank Jackson Matthews speaks as the honored guest at a 2015 Security Battalion dinner.

Honoring the past. Paying a visit to the Spotsylvania,
Virginia, Confederate cemetery and the grave of his
ancestor and Confederate war hero, Hugh Blakeney,
who was killed during the Civil War while serving
with the 8th South Carolina Infantry, C.S.A.

Ten

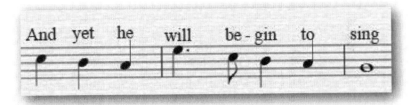

And yet he will be-gin to sing

Frank Jackson Matthews
The Four Seasons, A Touch of Spring

With the war over, the job of cleaning up began. Jack was sent to Pearl Harbor and assigned to assist the officers in surveying and selling the surplus military property that was left scattered across Asia. Jack traveled with six or seven colonels through the countries scattered in the pacific. Their mission was to make records of the sale of tanks, boats and all forms of equipment too bulky and expensive to return to the United States mainland.

The assignment was less exciting than Jack had hoped. He spent most of his time in a hotel room all but chained to a typewriter. The situation was not helped by the fact that Jack had no formal training in office work and typed with what he referred to as the, "Columbus style"...discover and land on it. Although at times he also called it his, "Biblical style"...seek and ye shall find. Rarely was he allowed to explore the exotic locales or even leave his hotel room. The war had come to an end and now everyone was in a rush to wrap up the loose ends and go home. In that regard, Jack was no exception.

Eventually the monotonous typing duty earned Jack enough service points to return home. In March of 1946 he headed back to the South, to his parents, and to his dreams of becoming a music professor. Before leaving Hawaii he put the finishing touches on his three-part piano concerto that had begun back with, *Anthurium*. He named the final piece, *Aloha*, the familiar Hawaiian greeting for both hello and goodbye. Symbolically, he was saying 'hello' to life after the war, and 'goodbye' to Hawaii. He named the entire set of work, *Maui Concerto,* in homage to his wartime island home.

Dear Mom and Dad,   August 31, 1945
    I've only had a few weeks to really enjoy Maui, but already it's time for "Aloha".
    We sailed out of the little harbor at Kahalui on a beautiful Saturday morning. There was a rainbow over Haiku, a remnant of an early morning shower. I remember when we returned to this harbor after the terrible battle of Iwo Jima. Transport after transport sailed in and debarked dirty battle-weary Marines. The local population assembled around the clock for three days and showered every truckload of Marines with flowers and ice cream.
    We have grown very close to these people, and Aloha is sad.
Love,
Jack

* * *

He wasted no time in using his GI bill to enroll in the University of North Carolina at Chapel Hill. His teacher and old friend, Mrs. Crosby Adams, had a good relationship with the head of the music department at the university and had recommended Jack for immediate admission to their program. Jack took every course he could, loading up with twenty to twenty-five credit hours each semester. Most students were limited to sixteen hours, but Jack's grades and dedication proved that he could handle the burden and so he was allowed ever increasing latitude by the university in creating his schedule. In addition to his music classes and general studies, he played the organ and piano for the university choir.

When the spring semester ended, and summer began, Jack and most of the other choir members went to work as cast members for *The Lost Colony* play on Roanoke Island, North Carolina. *The Lost Colony* play, which was staged each summer in the open-air *Waterside Theatre*, depicted a failed attempt by Queen Elizabeth, Sir Walter Raleigh, and a group of English colonists to establish a permanent settlement in the new world on the North Carolina coast. Within a couple years of its founding, the colony disappeared without a trace. Despite the mysterious disappearance of the settlement, this historical effort at colonizing the new world was celebrated each summer by generations of North Carolinians.

Some students would function as actors in the play while others handled the sets or other theatre related duties. They would rent rooms in the homes of locals and take their meals communally in the town's high school cafeteria. Jack enjoyed this arrangement greatly. The room he rented had a small patio that was surrounded by lush fragrant Gardenia bushes. Gardenias, he quickly determined, were a vast improvement from the smell of burning kerosene, or the rotten fragrance of five smelly tent mates.

Jack's particular assignment for the play was bringing the scenes to life with music on the theatre's large Hammond organ. The organ was the only musical accompaniment for the production. The instrument not only had to provide the sweeping scores and background melodies, but also the vivid sounds of the approach of the Queen, the swirling and crashing of the ocean voyage, and the pounding threat of encroaching Indians.

As Jack accompanied the dramatic tableaux on the big organ, he surveyed his fellow choir members' performances with a critical eye. For a summer troop they weren't half bad. Although, he really felt that the girl who played Queen Elizabeth had an appallingly thick southern accent that made her sound more like she should be the Queen of Savannah than of England.

His colleague Andy, who was also in the choir at the university, played Sir Walter Raleigh and, in Jack's estimation, did a pretty good job. Andy tended to be a serious fellow and very focused on promoting his acting career. He was pleasant and professional but generally kept more to his own pursuits than the rest of the players.

The play was a daytime production and Jack worked a second job playing piano and organizing a variety show at one of the two casinos on the island's coast. Locals and summer vacationers alike spent evenings at the casinos among the clatter of slot machines and the liberal flow of liquor. Jack considered his variety show to be a preferential option to either of those diversions and took no small measure of pride in its production. Many of the students cast in the play were already part of the university's musical comedy organization, *The Sound and Fury,* and so Jack had a cast of fairly experienced performers to pull from.

The variety shows were a resounding success and drew in crowds of summer vacationers for the casino owner's ultimate benefit. The show also gave Jack a benefit; the chance to practice his skills in producing a show to his own liking. Jack's friend Andy was also finding some success with his second job performing monologues at another casino. It was not until years later that Jack would see his university cohort reach the pinnacle of his success with another production, *The Andy Griffith Show.*

* * *

Graduation day from the University of North Carolina came in 1949. Jack finally had his music degree but still no masters degree to qualify him for teaching, and once again, no money to get one. He knew only one sure way to get money for his education, and that was to go right back into the Marine Corps. This time Jack would be stationed at Camp Lejeune and earning his commission as an officer. It wasn't long before he was once again put in the familiar position of playing the piano at the local officers club.

In the military it was the standard for formal names to be used in any official undertaking. So, during his tenure in the Marine Corps, the young Corporal, Frank Jackson Matthews, was always called by his legal and Christian name of "Frank."

The officers club was frequented by some of the fellas Jack had met as a university student at Chapel Hill. Many of them had left military service for university life but were now getting back into uniform as the war in Korea brought them out of academia and into their dress khakis. The men would come into the club for drinks and socializing. These old university pals knew the familiar pianist only as "Jack." During the unique collision of these two worlds Jack became accustomed to answering to greetings of either of his names.

It was not long into his training before the military's "Frank" had earned his commission as an officer. He was now a Lieutenant. As part of earning his commission, he was invited to an exclusive event, a reception for all newly commissioned officers hosted by the commanding general of the base. It was a traditional ceremonial part of earning a commission and every new officer wanted to make a good first impression.

The Marine Corps and its young officers followed a strict protocol of social obligation. Making a good first impression on the general, and the general's wife for that matter, was considered nearly as advantageous to one's military career as a medal pinned to your chest. Hence, on the night of the event every uniform was perfectly pressed and every head had a fresh haircut.

Jack and his newly commissioned pals stood somewhat stiff and uncomfortable in a loosely formed circle to the right side of the reception room. Past the piano, and beyond the table of delicately fashioned hors d'oeuvres, Jack spotted the general's wife winding through the crowd of officers. She moved lithely and with perfect poise and grace. As she encountered each new cluster of officers she would confidently offer a gloved hand to each young man followed by a few moments of polite and proper conversation. Statuesque and refined in her evening gown she circulated through the newly christened officers with ease. She was the epitome of everything Jack thought a general's wife should be. She was lovely, gracious, and with an air of shrewd wisdom about her which conveyed to the astute in the room that she was someone who took orders from no one, including, in all likelihood, the general himself.

It wasn't long before she crossed the room and walked confidently up to Jack. He felt several small beads of sweat form on his polished forehead. Addressing him as, "Lieutenant Matthews," she politely offered her hand of congratulation. Then she remarked:

"I've heard you playing at the officers club, you're quite good."

Jack was put at ease by her compliment and replied, "Yes Ma'am, thank you."

Tilting her head to the side and raising one eyebrow slightly, she posed a question to the fledgling officer: "I've noticed that some of the men at the club greet you as Frank, while others refer to you as Jack, what is your real name Mr. Matthews?"

Relieved at the simplicity of the question, without hesitation Jack boldly replied, "I'm Frank on base and Jack off."

To which the general's wife, both eyebrows raised in astonishment, and a small amused smirk on her face, replied: "My... you certainly are!"

Eleven

Frank Jackson Matthews
Comes the Forty-Niner

There was little time to dwell on his verbal blunder; Jack was ordered to Camp Pendleton, California to be a trainer. Although only twenty-four-years-old, he was combat experienced and every battle-seasoned Marine was needed to train the young grunts heading into the campaigns of Korea. At Camp Pendleton he trained young privates on weapons, tactics, and anything else that he was ordered to teach or that he thought might help keep them alive.

One part of standard training for the fresh Marines was practicing shore landings in a Higgins boat or *The Landing Craft, Personnel, Vehicle*, as it was formally titled. The vessel was nothing new to Jack; he was all too familiar with the rudimentary craft from his previous time in the Marines. The boats appearance was simplistic and utilitarian with an open cargo area thirty-six foot long, almost eleven feet wide, and capable of transporting thirty-six Marines directly onto a beach landing. The front end of the craft was a seven foot steel ramp and the rear of the boat held two .30 caliber machine guns.

While the craft was simple looking, its design was both timely and inspired. Historically, amphibious landings were centered on a port that would allow cumbrous ships to dock and unload large numbers of assault troops. Most ports, and particularly those of any military significance, were heavily fortified and defended. Large vessels wanting to breach an enemy harbor generally had to battle through a defenders best land and sea forces to secure any hope of incursion.

In contrast to large transport ships, Higgins boats were small and highly maneuverable and their clever construct eliminated the need for a man-made port. The boat's design allowed it to be driven onto a shoreline and its landing ramp dropped quickly, thus permitting troops to charge from its interior onto a beach landing zone. The overall result was that troops and supplies could be quickly ferried from ships anchored at sea onto any beach or other shallow water landing with tremendous efficiency, therefore avoiding the heavily defended harbors of the enemy.

The military recognized the boat's usefulness in the Second World War. It was used extensively, and infamously, in the landings at Normandy and Iwo Jima. The boats had such a heavy impact on the amphibious attack strategies in Europe and the Pacific that the Supreme Allied Commander, Dwight D. Eisenhower, declared that the Higgins boat had been the key to the Allied strategy and victory in the war. Jack could have argued it was the Marines.

Now, a decade later, the modern and preferred method of delivering troops was the helicopter. Unfortunately the reality was that helicopters were in short supply, as were both mechanics to work on them and trained pilots to fly them. So, for Lieutenant Matthews, it was back to training in his old friend the Higgins boat.

From the base at Camp Pendleton, Jack and the new recruits loaded into the boat for a routine training exercise. On one side of the swirling and rocking craft was the city of San Diego, on the other side stood the red spires of the Hotel Del Coronado, a glamorous beach resort best known for its grand architecture, luxurious amenities, and famous clientele.

The hotel was the toast of Hollywood elite and boasted among its notorious guests both the wealthy and the celebrated. Notables like aviator Charles Lindbergh, Wizard of Oz writer L. Frank Baum, and a few United States Presidents were among the elegant hotel's prominent guests. Many starlets and leading men of the stage and screen were also known to frequent the Del Coronado. It was fashionable for the hotel's luminaries to spectate and applaud at the military exercises taking place in the waters just beyond where they lolled beachside in the California sun.

The Higgins boat swirled and bounded through the bay waters as a number of bronzed and pampered royals of the California Coast watched with novelty from the beach of the Del Coronado.

The boat lurched and rattled forward as thick curtains of choking fumes whirled in the air and dusky waters bashed into the vessel's armored sides. Jack was holding on tight near the boat's weighty metal ramp and bracing himself against each slamming blow. Obviously out of practice with his driving skills, the coxswain turned a hard left and struck the beach at a disastrously wrong angle. In an instant the ramp shook loose with a roaring animalistic moan. Jack leaped over the side of the vessel just as an oncoming wave hit hard. The boat jerked with ferocity and struck a powerful blow to the back of his legs. The force of it was so strong that it lifted him from his position and ricocheted his flailing body back against the unyielding hull and then up into the air. He was hurled helplessly into the deep blue swirling waters. The last thing Jack recalled was seeing his left boot go flying into the depths of the sea, and then everything went dark…

Slowly, as if waking from a dream, he became aware that his head was being cradled in the warm lap of what must certainly be an angel of Heaven.

She was whispering to him in hushed soft tones… he couldn't make out what she was saying, but he knew instinctively that they were words of comfort and solace.

Was he dead? Was this Heaven? Was it a dream?

He felt safe and happy here in this state of foggy reality, as if he were surrounded by a tender mist that obscured his senses but simultaneously guarded his entire being. He tried to force his eyes to open wider but flowing shadows interspersed with flickers of blinding white light obscured his view of the cherub embracing his head.

Now he began to more clearly hear the soft whisperings as they came forth in a steady unabated stream.

"My brave boy, it's going to be just fine," the angel cooed in a silky deep voice.

He looked upward, straining to see all the glory that must certainly be shining around this angel. He could only see a duo of mammoth white clouds floating ever so closely just above his eyes and periodically blocking the flickering white light of heaven. He felt the warmth of the angel's radiance and her velvety fingers touched his hair in gentle consoling caresses.

Gradually his thoughts became sharper and his senses less vague. More and more he could discern other voices…men's voices…then he heard the distinct call of a gull… then the rhythmic sound of waves.

The light that now and again struck into the corner of his throbbing right eye was certainly that of the sun. As his vision began to come into focus he realized that the clouds drifting overhead were not the cumulous billows of the heavens, but the very earthly and flesh-colored bulbous orbs of men's dreams. His angel was of this world after all…though certainly those alabaster hillocks hovering above his face were nothing if not heavenly.

Without warning, and with distinct jarring swiftness, he was yanked upwards. Two pairs of stout hands were grasping him, one set clutching his shoulders and the other his ankles. The warmth fled from his body in a cold rush and the soothing words were gone from his ears. Worst of all, he was ripped from the sight of those glistening pale beacons of comfort and succor. He was dropped unceremoniously onto a hard canvas cot.

The cot was lifted into the air and began to move forward. His wet bruised body was jostled inhospitably as he was roughly carried across the sands to the back of a Navy ambulance. As the cot was lifted into the back of the waiting conveyance Jack raised his head in a desperate attempt to catch sight of his cherub.

There in the sand, being helped up from her ministering position on Coronado Beach was his angel, Ms. Jane Russell.

He never saw Ms. Russell again, or for that matter, his left boot.

Twelve

Ev' ry guy I know has a girl back home,

Frank Jackson Matthews
I Wonder Who's Waiting for Me

In 1953 the Korean War ended and Jack was free to return to his civilian life and his university dreams. Jack's parents had left South Carolina when his father was assigned to pastor a church in the small community of Zachary, Louisiana. Now Louisiana would be Jack's home as well.

Having acquired more education benefits through his service, Jack began earning his Masters degree in music history and composition at Louisiana State University in nearby Baton Rouge.

During the summer he took on the role of choir director at his father's church. It was a small white country church with a burgeoning congregation and a large and lively choir. For the young choir director, selecting music to match his father's sermon topics was the easy part; the hard part was keeping the choir contented.

There seemed to be no shortage of egos actively at work among the vocalists. The devil had his devious hand in the mix, using the old fashioned but effective tool of envy. If Jack assigned a solo to one woman then it was sure to make six others pout in resentment. Men and women who would never consider committing the sins of larceny or profanity would easily covet themselves into the dark prince's cloying grasp over the matter of a simple solo.

Father Matthew's biddings had to be folded into the preparation as well. Jack knew his father did not want to suspend his oratory through long performances of multi stanza operetta. He wanted the choir selections to be appropriate and well-performed of course, but most of all he wanted them to be brief.

Keeping choir and preacher content, while simultaneously producing a quality performance, were aspects of a choir director's work that few outside of the profession could really appreciate. At times Jack felt as if he alone was battling the devil to keep the choir on track.

One steamy summer evening he stood in the front of the church thumbing through some rather tattered pages of an old hymnal. Nothing in the selections was inspiring him today. He tossed the heavy volume with its worn green cover and yellowed pages to the side of his music stand. Internally he engaged himself in a somewhat heated debate on whether he should run through next Sunday's hymn list -getting its final practice done and out of the way- or start work on the new material he had selected for next month.

The following month's first service would include a challenging rendition of *Abide with Me: Fast Falls the Eventide* and three additional hymns motivated by his father's planned sermon on the biblical illustrations surrounding death. The selections happened to include several female solos and Jack dreaded the task of attempting to assign them without raising the ire of the particularly fussy soprano section.

As he continued his inner deliberations, the choir members walked to and fro among the wooden pews warming up their vocal cords or chatting affably. Several of the tenors had taken their places and were practicing the opening notes of next week's first hymn. Jack was unconsciously glancing toward the rear of the sanctuary when in through the doors of the church came a sable-haired beauty like none he had ever seen.

The girl was tall and lithe and sheathed tightly in a summer dress the color of dark red wine. Her face glistened with a dewy sheen courtesy of heavy humidity and the repressive southern heat. Patches of dark perspiration encircled the fabric of her dress anywhere it had lain against her ivory skin. Her eyes were dark and glimmering, like spheres of polished onyx. Her lips were the vivid pink of mandevilla petals. She walked toward the dais with the grace of a queen and Jack stared, his breath caught high in his throat and a bead of sweat forming near his neatly trimmed hairline.

An outgoing young woman from the Soprano section marched the girl straight up to where Jack stood, his mouth agape. The woman waved her hand dramatically in the air and smiling widely she announced:

"Director…everyone…everyone," her booming voice pealed through the sanctuary and brought them all to attention. "This is Margaret," the girl announced, "she is a wonderful alto, so please make her welcome."

The choir members immediately stepped forward in turn to welcome the new songstress. Jack gave the dark haired girl a brief nod and swallowed hard. He was acutely aware that he was now in the presence of the most beautiful woman he had ever seen.

* * *

Her full name was Margaret Gay Murphy, and she lived with her parents in nearby Baker, Louisiana. Her father was the strong and respected Thomas Wesley Murphy, or "T.W." as the men of the church called him, and her mother, the very proper and serious, Rosalie Murphy.

During choir practices Jack did his best not to stare. From among the multitude of voices he could discern hers singing each note with a distinctive abandonment that reminded him of sunshine and joy. During breaks in rehearsals he would watch her visiting with the other women. She had dancing dark eyes and a freely given laugh that were music to his senses.

She was radiant.

Through discreet inquiry, and some surreptitious listening to the prattle of the choir, Jack learned that Margaret was in the long process of divorcing her husband, a rare occurrence in rural and religious Louisiana. More surprising was that Margaret was the mother to a beautiful baby girl named Madeline. She was a happy and effervescent child who possessed both her mother's twinkling eyes and her easy laugh.

Margaret's soon to be ex-husband was by all accounts an unbalanced traveling salesman who disappeared for months at a time without satisfactory explanation and did nothing to support young Margaret or her little girl. The one single support check that the charlatan had sent for baby Madeline's care immediately bounced and the fellow was never heard from again.

Gradually, Jack worked up the courage to speak to Margaret more and more often. Before long, Margaret reciprocated the interest. However, Rosalie Murphy made it clear that she would not allow her daughter to date another man, even a minister's son, while her marriage was still legally intact. After all, even if the circumstances Margaret found herself in were beyond her control, a goodly amount of propriety was to be observed.

Slowly and steadily Jack gained a bit of grudging and conditional approval from the Murphy family. Dating for Jack and Margaret was partly exhilarating and partly exasperating. Courting was a chance for Jack to spend time with the object of his affection but that time always included the watchful and wary eye of mother Rosalie, and at times, Margaret's six opinionated aunts. For a solid year Jack and Margaret's time together consisted only of sitting and talking quietly together in the living room of the Murphy home, with Rosalie and T.W. monitoring the situation warily from the very next room. Occasionally ugly rumors would circulate through the community about Margaret's marital status or Jack's decision to court a divorced woman. Jack simply ignored them. The patience and determination that he had cultivated through the younger years of his life now paid their dividends. He bore the scrutiny like the tireless student and soldier he had always been. His mind and his heart stayed focused on Margaret and no extenuating circumstances, social demands, or family uncertainties would deter him.

On June 1, 1958, Jack and Margaret stood in the front of a small white country church in Zachary, Louisiana. Jack's father stood opposite the couple, Bible in hand, and his mother sat in the long wooden front pew in her finest Sunday dress. Margaret wore a pink suit.

When Father Curtis finished his discourse, Margaret took Jack's hand and said quietly, "I love you Mr. Matthews."

In that moment Jack knew that these were the best and most important words he had ever heard, or ever would hear. Jack had finally and formally won the hand of his beauty. She was now and *forever* his bride.

Jack, Margaret, and baby Madeline moved into a small home that he had purchased for them in nearby Baton Rouge. By now he had earned his long-awaited master's degree in music from Louisiana State University and in September of 1959 their family grew when a baby girl, Janet Gay, was born. Janet was a serious and thoughtful child who everyone recognized as being possessed with her mother's striking good looks and her father's bright and curious mind.

Things were also going well for Jack professionally. He secured a coveted role as a teaching assistant at the university and began planning for the day that he would achieve a fulltime professorship. His academic dreams were finally in arms reach.

Within the music department the professors were grudgingly being pulled into the new age. The central library asked each division to convert their records into the university's new mainframe computer system. The very tenured and reticent professors that made up the department had absolutely no knowledge of, or interest in, the new-fangled world of computers. They had no intention of expending any time studying the, "*confounded machines,*" at this stage of their careers. In their learned minds, the logical solution to the problem was simply to assign the task to the lowest ranking faculty member. So, off Jack went to the library to learn the new world of computer languages.

Regardless of the utilitarian nature of the task he was currently assigned to, the assistant teaching job constituted a crucial step in reaching his ultimate aspirations. However, on its own that role was not providing enough income to support a growing family and a home and Jack took any and all extra work he could find. He taught piano lessons in private homes, joined the Army reserves, and continued to lead the church choir. He formed a small orchestra of about six guys that periodically played at the Baton Rouge Country Club or wherever they could find a bit of work.

He picked up some regular work on a local television show called, *Date on 28.* The show was hosted by local celebrity, Bob Peters. The gregarious host would interview various resident notables or any arrant movie star who happened to be passing through the area. Jack provided the live musical entertainment in between each of the shows planned segments. Generally he would play songs from the current hit-parade or whatever popular music the management requested. The host, Peters, would say: "Take it away Jack," and while Jack played, the staff would scramble around to get ready for the next interview.

He also got a part-time job in the Governor's office working on the state's computers as a systems analyst. Here was where his time being forced into learning computer programming at the university now paid off by paying the bills.

Keeping up with all the various jobs was getting complicated, and things at home were getting even more complicated. Jack's daughters were healthy and growing, but his bride Margaret was frequently sickly and bedridden. Margaret battled a slew of indeterminate respiratory illnesses. During each episode of illness she would grow weaker and paler with each passing day until finally pneumonia would set in and she would be sent to the hospital. Bouts of hospitalization, sometimes for a month or more at a time, did not come cheap and Jack struggled with worry about finances. Most of all he worried about Margaret's ability to endure her ever increasing frailty. Her physician felt certain that it was the dense moist atmosphere of the Deep South keeping her lungs in a continuous state of struggle. A move to a dryer climate might just help restore her to health. The doctor recommended an immediate departure for the dryer climates of the West. He suggested Arizona or California. Jack was stunned at the dramatic prescription. To make such a drastic move, to so far away, with no money and two small daughters would be a serious undertaking. There were a number of considerations, after all, both of their families were here in Louisiana and Jack finally had his teaching assistant job at the university. The job was his first tenuous step on the path to becoming a full-fledged professor of music.

He wasn't the only one with concerns. Margaret's family had voiced their clear and unwavering objections to the move. Upon hearing the extraordinary prescription, Margaret's mother objected most strenuously of all. In fact, the entire family reacted rather poorly to the idea and was generally disinclined to support any plan that took her away from Louisiana. It was too far away. It was too far from the family. There were too many unknowns. Where would they live? Where would he work? What if it wasn't safe? Who would help care for the children? Home and family, they declared, could provide for her best and that was that.

The more Jack and the doctor insisted that the move be considered, the more furiously Margaret's family resisted. Finally, believing time to be of the essence, the impatient doctor visited the family at home. He explained in no uncertain terms to T.W. that either Margaret could move out west, or the family could move her to a plot of land at the local cemetery. Rosalie still wanted to object, but as the head of the family T.W. declared that they would support the move if that was indeed what the doctor and Jack thought best.

Jack sat alone and considered his bride, pallid and weak from continuous ailments. Maybe everyone else was right, maybe they should just stay put and keep fighting Margaret's illness one bout at a time. Jack had been a disciplined fighter his whole life. He fought through the dark sepulcher-like atmosphere of the church to study piano, he fought his father to join the military, he fought the enemy on Iwo, and he fought for every dollar he needed to earn his music degree. But now, watching Margaret listless and pale, failing to thrive day by day in the humid air of south Louisiana, he came to a new realization. This time standing and fighting would not work…this time he would have to run.

Thirteen

Sil - ent ships sail by strange rock pyr - a -mids.

Frank Jackson Matthews
Memorabilia from Iwo Jima: Prelude

As old dreams faded into the background, new as-pirations took shape. Jack's focus sighted itself unswervingly on finding a way for his family to move to the dryer climate of the West. With no savings, and little chance of securing a teaching job at a university where he was not known or connected, Jack began ap-plying for *any* job that would get the family out of south Louisiana.

One day, on his way into work at the University, he grabbed a trade publication that was distributed out of New Orleans. Within its inky pages was an advertisement placed by a company called Lockheed Missiles and Space Company. The announcement included the date and time of open interviews being held the following week in New Orleans. It specifically called for men trained in computers and able to immediately move out West.

Jack, wearing his best summer suit, arrived at the interview punctual and prepared. He learned that the Lockheed Missiles and Space Company had secured a government contract to work on the Poseidon missile system and they needed programmers to work at their Sunnyvale, California center. The Poseidon missile was going to be the second in a series of long-range Navy rockets with nuclear warheads. When finished, the Poseidon would be 34 feet in length and weigh almost 65,000 lbs. The missile would be able to travel a distance of 2,500 Kilometers and deploy multiple warheads to different locations. Its predecessor, the Polaris, had a similar engine design system, but lacked the accuracy and delivery capabilities that the Navy sought to achieve with this new advanced version.

The salary was decent, and more importantly, the company would pay to move the family to California. Jack agreed to sign a three-year contract and was hired on the spot.

* * *

Grudgingly, Margaret's family helped them pack and load their modest belongings into the moving truck that had been hired and paid for by the company. The truck, now half full with the Matthew's household items, lurched to life and departed. The truck would continue on its journey on to pick up another new employees home goods and bric-a-brac and then rendezvous with them in California in a week's time.

Jack, Margaret, and the two girls piled into their Dodge 6-cylinder station wagon and left the humid air of south Louisiana - and everything else familiar to them - behind. When they rolled through West Texas Margaret suddenly breathed clear and deep, in a way she had not done in months, or maybe years. By the time they crossed the California line she was nearly the picture of perfect health. Jack felt a wave of relief; he had made the right decision after all. The family pulled into a modest motel on El Camino Real that would be their home for the next week courtesy of the Lockheed Missiles and Space Company.

Jack had arranged to lease a house for the family beginning the following week and the furniture truck was due to arrive just in time for them to move in. Since he had to report to work right away, the task of finalizing the lease and meeting the movers would fall to Margaret.

The leased house was in the town of Los Gatos. While Jack was at his first day of work, Margaret went to the new house to meet the moving truck and sign the paperwork. As she pulled into the drive of the small shabby home, the movers sat in the cab of their truck anxiously waiting to unload. On the crumbling front porch steps of the home stood the presumptive landlord, a set of lease papers in hand. Margaret had never seen anyone quite like him back in Louisiana. The man was dressed in a garish polyester suit, his hair was greasy and dark and slicked up into a peak on the top of his head. A cigarette hung from one corner of his mouth and where he gripped its yellowed filter Margaret could see several brown and broken teeth. Margaret felt her throat tense up a bit and a queasy feeling developed in her stomach. Something about this man and this situation made her instinctively uneasy. She pushed down the jitters in her stomach as the man fingered the stack of papers awaiting her signature.

Jack had struck a deal to pay $175 a month for the house. The grubby-man's paperwork gave a much higher amount of $250 a month, an amount that would stretch the family's budget to nearly the breaking point. The corner of the man's mouth worked into a small snarl and his esurient eyes narrowed down into black marbles of silky darkness as he matter-of-factly stated his opinion that the property was worth more than they originally agreed to.

Margaret stood frozen in momentary confusion at this change of events. The man continued on with his reasoning and as he talked his voice took on a sickly patronizing tone. He explained that in his estimation Margaret had little choice in the matter, after all, the movers were already there, waiting impatiently … *and her husband was not*. It seemed obvious to Margaret that this loathsome character supposed she was the quintessential helpless female, willing to follow the direction and urging of any man, particularly when under the duress of time and circumstance.

He pressed the papers and the pen into her and his face hardening he said:

"Come on lady; just sign…just sign 'em." Each time he spoke his voice grew more hard-edged and his manner more forceful. "Just sign 'em, they're waitin' lady," he waved a hand toward the moving truck parked on the street with its engine idling.

Margaret's brown eyes flashed with anger and her face flushed with a surge of heat. She felt suddenly strong, stronger than she had been in months, maybe even years. Her physical illness had abated. She had climbed and conquered the mountains that were her family's fearful objections to the move as well as her own trepidation. Now, standing in the street in Los Gatos California, this one sad excuse for a man was not going to ruin their new start. Her instinct was to slap him, to curse his very being as she left in a huff and never looked back. Her rational side reminded her that the company had only agreed to pay for a week at a hotel. She was in a foreign place and thoroughly without money or resources until Jack received his first paycheck, still a full two weeks away. Feelings of fear and hesitation crept swiftly into her conscious, undermining her confidence. She needed to know what Jack wanted her to do. They were a team, and right now she needed him.

At his new desk in the Lockheed building, Jack sat shuffling through some first day material he had been given to review and thinking somewhat dreamily about the start of their new life in California. The room he sat in was fairly large and utilitarian. In it were fifty to seventy-five rectangular metal desks lined up in neat rows. Each desk held a phone and a few neatly bound manuals. Jack noticed that some of the desk's toward the front of the room also held novel style books – biographies, history books, and even some stories by Zane Grey. At nearly every desk a man sat quietly reading. Jack thumbed through the large employee binder he had been given and imagined Margaret and the girls unpacking and arranging their belongings in their new home.

Unexpectedly his desk phone jingled. It woke him with a start from the dreamy and pensive state he had been enjoying. On the other end of the line, Margaret frantically explained the situation with the greasy man and his stack of papers. As Jack listened to his bride's description of the charlatan's demands, his face grew hotter. His normally composed and orderly thoughts began to bubble and sear like acid boiling in a cauldron.

A frustrated Margaret finished her hurried tale and paused. She took a shallow breath and awaited her husband's reply. If she had doubted her initial instincts in the matter, her determination was buoyed by Jack's uncharacteristic, and unmistakably livid, response, "TELL HIM TO GO SCREW HIMSELF!" he bellowed into the Lockheed end of the phone.

Margaret hung up the receiver without further discussion. She looked the man straight in the eyes and in her own, slightly more ladylike - but certainly not weaker - manner, she told the would-be landlord to, "*go pound sand!*" The man stood slack jawed as Margaret dropped the papers to the floor, turned, and strode away indignantly. The beady-eyed huckster would have to swindle some other suckers; the Matthews were not going to play his game.

* * *

The first few weeks at Lockheed drifted by without incident. Jack and his co-workers had been given some standard orientation materials to review and a few manuals to read quietly at their desks. The pace was painfully slow but Jack wasn't going to complain, after all, the company had kindly agreed to pay for additional time at a hotel and to store their household items. As it turned out, the extension of time hadn't been needed. Margaret had demonstrated her determination and found them another house to rent the very next day.

As the third and fourth week passed Jack became increasingly restless and eager to start the real work that he was brought there for. He couldn't for the life of him understand why he had not yet been given a programming assignment. Finally, bored into action, he summoned the courage to ask a supervisor when the real work, the computer work, would be starting. The response was a pleasant but abrupt order to, "sit down, stay out of the way, and keep your mouth shut."

Jack didn't understand. He wasn't the only one puzzled; the other recently arrived men were equally perplexed, and equally bored. Some of them started talking quietly to the guys that had been there awhile. One ruddy-faced young man who had been employed for almost five months motioned surreptitiously to Jack and several others. Calling them over with a silent gesture of his hand, he gathered the newcomers into a makeshift huddle near a few empty desks in a quiet corner of the room. The man kept his voice to a whisper and glanced around furtively as he spoke. "Look buddy," he addressed the man standing closest to him on the right, "the work is done, see...there's nothing for us to do."

He stopped talking and looked at the men as if these statements should provide a complete and acceptable understanding to all present. The men, now even more bewildered, continued to stare and wait for further explanation.

The stealthy man took one more cautious glance around the room and then continued on. This time he went through the whole meghilla, from the beginning. The missile it seemed was all but completed. In order for Lockheed to get paid by the government, the company's work contract had to be fulfilled as written. Fulfilling the contract meant employing a certain number of men for the next three years, despite their being little to nothing left for them to do.

Jack had never heard of such a thing and didn't know quite what to make of it. He wasn't sure he totally believed the young man's bizarre explanation. Whatever was going on, he couldn't afford to leave this job…he had committed himself, both by signing a contract and by bringing his family to this new frontier of the American dream. Paying back the moving expense money and scrambling to find a new job was not a realistic solution. Having to return to Louisiana, and hence return to Margaret's medical troubles, was simply not an option for the young husband and father of two growing girls. Still, sitting there doing next to nothing for three whole years was not a greatly palatable option either.

Jack sat back down at his desk and began to once again thumb through and study the manuals he had been given as if he were actually going to have to use them. Weeks passed, or more accurately stated the weeks dragged by. The men grew tired of reading, swapping jokes, and staring at the clock. Finally Jack and a few others asked if they could take on a community volunteer project to pass the time. The company heartily agreed and even offered to help locate the project work. Jack was excited. Maybe it wasn't exactly what he'd signed up for, but any work was better than sitting around feeling as useful as a pirogue without a paddle.

The first project was a perfect match for Jack's university roots. He developed a computerized system for student registration for San Jose State University. The next project was organizing into a coherent computer system the fiscal records for the state of Alaska Highway Department. The federal government had a host of new regulations that required each state to have their highway records in an easily auditable computer program. Lockheed held a rapidly aging contract to build such a system for Alaska. It was a contract that was at significant risk of default. Either by coincidence or providence, Jack was familiar with these regulations from his work on computers back in the Louisiana Governor's office. He suggested that they obtain a copy of that state's program and simply change all Louisiana references to Alaska. The plan worked and the contract was fulfilled. Alaska was happy, the Feds were happy, and Lockheed was happy. Jack got a one hundred dollar bonus. Other community projects followed and he was able to have all the useful work he wanted as he completed his commitment to Lockheed.

Fourteen

Frank Jackson Matthews
California, My Home

When the Lockheed contract ended, the men were released from their obligation. Work in the field of music and music teaching seemed to be particularly scarce. To pay the bills, Jack took a job on the north side of San Francisco in the computer department at the Fireman's Fund Insurance Company. Jack once again found himself working on computers as he supervised training on the large mainframes. There was a long daily commute of well over an hour each way to and from the family's home in San Jose. In Jack's mind it was always a temporary job. He was still dreaming of a career in music. When the company announced that they were moving the operation further north to Marin County, an almost impossible commute, Jack saw his opportunity to leave and once again pursue his dream.

To that end he took a job teaching piano at Steven's Music Store which had three locations in Santa Clara County. The work was enjoyable, but the store kept nearly half of everything he made. Frustrated with only taking home a fraction of the money he was earning, he sat down and studied a map of the area. He calculated that if he scheduled his route carefully he could teach all of his students in their own homes, at their preferred times, and double his income. Instead of parents driving their children to a store for lessons, the teacher was conveniently coming to them. The mothers loved it. He accommodated appointments from six am to eight pm. Jack was able to teach as much as he wanted and his roster of students grew. The more he taught, the more he learned about how to get and keep his students engaged. He began to create special arrangements that made it easier for different levels of students to not only play the music, but to play the styles of music they were actually interested in. His methods were successful and by word of mouth alone he quickly amassed enough students to generate a full schedule of pupils and a demanding work week.

Jack was working in music full time but still not achieving his dream of being a university teacher. He had tried getting hired at a few institutions but his timing could not have been worse. The state was tightening its budget for colleges and no one was hiring. He decided to try a more circuitous route to getting his foot in the door. At nearby Foothills College in Los Altos, he volunteered to arrange some music for the chorale group, the *Fanfares*. The group was quite talented and performed all over the state of California. Jack thought that maybe…just maybe…arranging music for the *Fanfares* would draw enough attention to get him a college teaching job. At the very least, the performance might generate some interest in what he considered to be his musical masterpiece, the *Iwo Jima Opus*.

After months of planning and practice with the talented group of collegiates, the date for the performance was set. The timing proved to be nothing less than a disaster. Vietnam War protests were breaking out all over the state and one particularly vocal group of self-proclaimed *hippies* had gotten word that music based on the battle of Iwo Jima was going to be publicly performed. The group quickly began making threats about disrupting the performance. Endangering innocent students and allowing the event to be turned into a circus was not a very palatable option. Jack was not happy, in fact he was rather perturbed about the turn of events but, there wasn't much choice; he scrapped the plan to have the students perform the Opus. Other, less contentious, music would need to go in its place. He sketched out a series of songs celebrating California and its history. Despite Jack's disappointment at the last minute change, the new material and its performance were a success. But, either because of the economy, or the unseen hand of the deity's greater plan, his work at Foothills College never led to the opportunities Jack had hoped for.

As a family, Jack and Margaret had now settled firmly into life as Californians and were enjoying the fruits of life in the Golden State. Those years seemed to drift by in idyllic fashion with all the normalcy and flurry of activity typical of a suburban family's life. It was truly the gilded age of California living for young families and for Jack and Margaret. The girls were healthy and growing and Margaret remained vibrant and well with none of the breathing issues that had plagued her back home in the sultry south. While Jack's wages were modest, it was enough to provide basic comforts and entertainments for the family.

Both Jack and Margaret prized the lifestyle of the area. In the evenings they would sit in the backyard surrounded by the verdant green of tropical plants and the smells of night blooming Jasmine and citrus. Jack would open a bottle of wine from the nearby Napa Valley and they would share the details of their day and their hopes for tomorrow.

The California lifestyle was a vibrant and active one for the young family. During the week there was school for the girls, chores for Margaret, and Jack's long hours at work. On the weekends there were wonderful sights and sounds to partake in. On some Saturdays the joyful couple would take their girls to the Santa Cruz Wharf and join the happy crowds walking on the long board-walk full of fabulous foods and amusements. Bowls of seafood chowder, the crashing of the ocean waves and the laughter of the girls were blissful. Other times they would go down to Monterey Bay for beach exploring and clam digging, to Sunset Beach north of Santa Cruz for a swim, or to the Henry Cowell Redwood forest for peaceful walks among the towering giants of the forest.

The couple was fond of trips to the wine county and its ubiquitous wine tastings; Jack preferred the dry selections and Margaret favored the sweet dessert wines. They both cherished the fresh fish and produce afforded by living near the pacific coast and would frequently dine on Hawaiian Spearfish, Chilean Sea Bass, and all manner of local succulent produce from nearby outdoor markets.

As the girls grew and became more independent, Jack and Margaret were able to travel further and more often. One year the couple decided to take a dream cruise around the Hawaiian Islands. Before boarding the ship in Oahu, Jack wanted to make a stop in Pearl Harbor and visit the site of the Arizona memorial.

The first time Jack had seen the remains of the USS Arizona was in 1945, just a few short years after the attack. Now returning on vacation with Margaret in 1989 the scene had changed dramatically. There was a visitor's center, plaques and informational signs, and even a gift shop. The surroundings had changed, but all that the downed ship represented had not. Over the last several decades Jack had tried to forget the war, for a long time he had not wanted to remember. Now it all flowed back. He remembered what it felt like to arrive in Hawaii, to survive the battle on Iwo, to live at Camp Maui. Finally, he recalled the day in August when the men had received word that Truman had dropped the bombs on Hiroshima and Nagasaki. He remembered feeling relieved. Tokyo Rose had been informing them nightly that the Japanese Kamikazes were planning death for them all when they invaded the mainland. In the years that followed the war he had heard much pity for the *thousands* that were killed in the explosions. Jack's perspective on the bombs had always been a little different, probably because he thought of the *millions* that would have surely died in the alternative land invasion...and because one of the dead would have almost certainly been him.

The cruise sailed to Maui; a stop Jack was greatly looking forward to. From the port in Kahului harbor, Jack and Margaret left the ship and went on an extensive tour of the island that had once been his home. They made special stops at all his old haunts, including, and most importantly, the site of old Camp Maui. The Camp was long gone, replaced by a memorial park. What was once training grounds and tents was now baseball fields, playgrounds, and picnic areas. A large central memorial highlighted the major campaigns of the Fourth Division, including Iwo Jima. Flying above it all were the Stars and Stripes. Jack paused to read a plaque honoring his Marine Corps brothers and his old Division Commander, General Cates. He looked around at the hills and slopes of the land and remembered the time so long ago when he sat in his tent and wrote songs about Iwo Jima. He thought about the mud and the training and how he had been so relieved to finally go home, and yet sad at the prospect of leaving this beautiful island. He thought about his old friend Sergeant Ahlin, someone he had not thought about in years. Ahlin had been the Fourth Division's mail Sergeant and the only man in the battle of Iwo to get up a functioning postal tent. Jack had helped him with what little time he had in between patrols. All the divisions had ended up using the tent to get their mail out. What had happened to his friend after the battle, Jack never knew.

* * *

Back on the ship in Kahului harbor it was talent night, and Jack agreed to play the piano. He sat down at the large instrument in the ship's grand showroom. It was wall to wall full of both passengers and crew members; there must have been over eight hundred people in the room. He looked around at the expectant faces and felt the tentacles of anxiety begin to creep into his stomach. What if they didn't like the piece…or the playing? He could easily perform a medley of the day's popular songs, or even a few old show tunes. Either of those choices would surely be well received. He had something special in mind. He played, *Aloha*, the final movement of the piano concerto he had written right there on Maui so many years ago. It was the very piece that he had written to say both 'hello' to the end of the war, and 'goodbye' to his island home. When he had finished, the passengers and crew of the cruise ship, the S.S. Constitution, gifted him with a round of rousing applause that he would never forget.

Fifteen

But Ruth said, "Entreat me not to leave
you or to return from following you; for
where you go I will go, and where you lodge
I will lodge; your people shall be my people,
and your God my God; where you die I
will die, and there will I be buried. May
the Lord do so to me and more also even
if death parts me from you. Ruth 1:16

Margaret's death was as sudden as her appearance in that Louisiana church so many years before. It was February of 1999 and in one moment Margaret and Jack were enjoying a peaceful California evening and the next she was simply crumpled in his arms and gone.

Jack decided that her memorial would not be a protracted line of mourners passing by an earthly shell. She would not lie in a cold casket, in a sterile funeral home.

The memorial would be like Margaret, full of beauty, adventure, laughter, and the joy of life.

In celebration of her life, family and friends gathered to toast her with champagne in the Redwoods that she so loved. Then they walked together in her honor on the laughter-filled wharf in Santa Cruz, just as she and Jack had done so many times.

And finally, in a style befitting a grand lady, Margaret's ashes were taken out to sea aboard a grand ship. Jack stood, silent and stoic on the helm of the elegant vessel with its formally dressed captain and crew at attention.

The vessel rocked back and forth in the waters of the sea and the music of Andrea Bocelli, the Italian tenor, resounded through the ship's loudspeakers. The song was *Con Te Partiro, A Time to Say Goodbye,* or more accurately translated from its original Italian, *I will leave with you.*

As the celebrants silently reflected, their hearts bursting with equal amounts of sadness for what they had lost and gratitude for the time they had been given, Margaret's ashes were scattered into the rolling waves. Each in their turn, the mourners cast into the sea a handful of flowers - lilies, tulips, roses…

The flowers were fitting symbols of Margaret's life, a life of spirited femininity. Against the darkness of the swirling waters the petals were as colorful and as strikingly lovely as the woman they accompanied into eternity.

Sixteen

All is gray and nos - tal- gic.

Frank Jackson Matthews
A Song for November

And so Jack began his life as a widower. He just couldn't stay in the same home, in the same town; it would never feel right without Margaret there. He considered his options. Oldest daughter Madeline was nearby in San Jose, and Janet was all the way on the east coast. Moving nearer to Janet in the East was just going too far, he wasn't ready to leave the West. Of course, staying near Madeline would mean no change at all...*he needed a change.* Jack had some cousins in Reno, and he could teach piano anywhere. Reno, Nevada, "The Biggest Little City in the World," became his next destination.

As it had been throughout his life, his instincts kept moving him toward music and teaching. There were always children waiting to learn piano or, more accurately stated, parents wanting their children to learn piano. It didn't take long for Jack to find a few students in the area. Then, when a local high school approached him with the need for an interim band director he jumped at the chance. Teaching the kids was a good diversion from thinking about his old life. Not that he was trying to completely block it out - Margaret's unending joy for life still inspired him daily, even in the moments of darkness that sometimes accompanied her physical absence.

But, it was in the evenings, after the hustle and bustle of the busy school day had faded, that his thoughts drifted back through his treasured years with his bride. He would always feel their years had been too few. They had certainly been filled with one adventure after another. He fondly recalled their many weekend trips to Lake Tahoe. Margaret would always put aside ten dollars to use for playing the slot machines, and Jack would make reservations for a restaurant and a show. On one particular trip he recalled how his white Datsun B210 had cruised easily through the twists and turns of Route 88. In the sporty car, they climbed up the Sierras to the picturesque mountain towns that straddled the California and Nevada line.

Jack bought the small four-speed after the girls had graduated from school and moved out on their own. It was a sunny and dry day; the perfect day for a drive to Tahoe, and the perfect conditions for testing out the power and performance of his recent purchase. In the rearview mirror he spotted another sports car easily navigating the tight curves of the rising mountain road and running up on him fast. Within seconds the other car roared past in a flash and disappeared around the next corner. "*Show-offs,*" thought Jack to himself. A mile ahead the car was back in sight. They seemed to be the only two cars for miles around; a pair of lone mavericks eating up the road. Sunlight flickered through the tall pines on either side of them as the way climbed steadily. The cars twisted to the right and then back to the left again up through the steep Carson Pass. Jack pushed on the gas pedal and accelerated into a short straight-away. As the other driver geared down for an upcoming curve, Jack saw his opportunity. He moved into the left lane and flew past the braggart. Margaret laughed with delight and waved a friendly greeting to the other car as they overtook it. The victory was short lived. The show-off closed in again and soon took the lead. Jack couldn't help admiring the car which looked to be a real beauty …and real expensive. Back and forth the two cars passed one another in a fun and friendly game as they climbed through the winding roads of the California Sierras. On the final brief straightaway Jack was in the lead when the other car made a final pass. This time the car slowed to match the speed of the Datsun and for several moments the cars ran side by side. Jack turned his head to smile and wave at his fellow travelers. To his surprise, in the car next to him, waving back and smiling, were Allen Ludden and his wife, Betty White.

Recollections of his life with beautiful Margaret were the happiest of memories. He cherished each one, but dared not dwell on them. He must move forward, always taking the memories with him as fortifying companions. He thumbed through some of his old compositions looking for something to work on for a while. Among his collection he noticed an old friend, the piece of chorale music he had written years before for the *Fanfares*. It was 1973 when Jack had first hurriedly composed the series of musical pieces for the Foothills College chorus. The collection included five distinct songs that traced the history of California from the arrival of the Spanish Conquistadores to the state's Centennial in 1950. Jack studied the collection and decided it was time that the pieces received a full orchestration.

He started with the first piece, the *CONQUISTADOR*. The song illustrated the Native's encounters with Spanish horseman on the shores of San Diego Bay. The sound of a trumpet announced the arrival of the Spaniards, their heads held high with regal pride and arrogance. The piece moved forward with new instruments joining in to reflect a sense of mystery in searching for storied cities of gold and of natives watching the arrival of these silver clad warriors with equal amounts or curiosity and apprehension. Were they the envoys of the mythical queen Califa? Would their guns and horses bring glory? ... Or would they bring death? As Jack's mind imagined the scenes he reflexively heard the instruments that accompanied them. When he was certain he had captured the intensity of those early explorations he moved on to the next period of California history.

Piece number two spoke to the founding of Christian missions in California and was simply titled, *KYRIE*. Kyrie was a reference to the sung prayer heard in liturgical masses and Gregorian chants. The composition followed the work of the Franciscan Monk, Father Junipero Serra, as he founded the first missions in California. The piece possessed a tone of somber formality and a chant-like quality. It was an appropriate nod to the diligence and reverence of the monks who inspired it. The oft heard prayer *Kyrie eleison* translates to *Lord, have mercy*. Mercy was certainly sought by Father Serra as he intrepidly confronted this untamed new territory.

The third selection in the series was, *MEMORIES FROM MONTEREY,* a look at the uniquely Spanish culture of the developing area. After explorers declared the region to be the property of Spain, four military districts, or presidios as the Spaniards called them, were established including the Monterey presidio. It was a volatile period in the history of California marked by daring explorations, trade skirmishes, conflicts with native peoples, and the struggles of Spanish soldiers to settle homesteads. Jack's orchestration of the period captured the sweeping beauty of the land and the Spanish people's passionate emotions. The piece was a full and rich one, heavily laden with both joy and sorrow.

Next, Jack musically heralded the arrival of the Gold Rush era in, *COMES THE FORTY-NINER.* Rollicking and hopeful rhythms evoked the yearning of the pioneer spirit to search out golden glory in the sun and dirt of the California territory. Like the men who crossed the prairies in covered wagons and climbed the Sierras, the music moved along in a determined manner, in moments lighthearted, and in others serious and resolute.

The final composition, *CALIFORNIA, MY HOME,* was the longest and grandest of the series. It not only spoke to the first one hundred years of California statehood, but it spoke to Jack on a personal level. California had been his home. Capturing all he loved about it seemed nearly impossible; the sunset beaches and snowy mountains, the starry nights and forest streams, the swallows of Capistrano and the poppies growing in the sands. Jack orchestrated the piece to convey the happy feelings of state pride and jubilation, along with a sense of sentimentality and humble gratitude to God.

When working on the series back in 1973 he had written it for only a mixed chorus along with trumpet and guitar solos. The pieces had been collectively titled, *California Heritage.* Now as a fully orchestrated Opus he could complete the title, *The Poppy in the Sand: A Symphonic History of California.*

He carefully cataloged the pieces among his collection of writings and went back to focusing on his band students.

He had only been in Reno for two short years when the interim band director position ended. It felt to Jack like a natural ending to this phase of life, as if it too had been an interim position. He had gone just far enough away from San Jose to separate from the life he had loved so much with Margaret, but not so far away as to be totally estranged from it. Maybe the decision to move had been made in haste…in the fog of grief. In the back of his mind he had hoped, believed even, that there were college teaching opportunities in Nevada that just didn't exist in California. That belief had been misguided and he had soon realized that the market for college teaching was just as tight and impossible to break into in Reno, as it had been in San Jose. His time there had left him financially strained and emotionally ready for something else. It truly had been an interim in his life; a time to reflect, to heal, and to prepare for whatever was to come. The impulse to move on was undeniable ...but to where, or what, he was not certain.

Daughter Janet and her husband, Rich, lived in Maryland. The youngest Matthews daughter had asked her father to move in with the couple several different times since Margaret's passing. It was the sensible thing to do. Jack had hesitated; he certainly didn't want to be a burden and he valued his independence. After a few rather heated back and forth discussions, it was settled. Son-in-law Rich flew to Reno and helped pack Jack's few personal items. They loaded up his rather old and beat-up Honda wagon and headed out. As the wagon rolled toward the east coast, Jack finally said goodbye to his life out West.

After arriving in Maryland he found a little work as a substitute music teacher and began the, sometimes painful, process of acclimating to daily life in his daughter's home. Janet's youngest son was about to start high school and having a teenager and a senior citizen both packed into a small house proved to be rife with every-day challenges for all involved. Everyone, including Jack, was more than ready for a new place with more space. Jack volunteered to help the family find a new home and with Janet's, "must have," list in hand he began the preliminary search.

In nearby Virginia, Stafford County was one area that Janet had kept her eye on for years now. Its history-packed and picturesque towns gave the area a lot of appeal. Jack searched the real estate listings and found the perfect place for them; several rural acres, just minutes from town, with a good high school, and a semi-private apartment style suite on the homes lower level. The rest of the family agreed, and just like that, Virginia was his new home.

Jack sat in his new basement apartment studying a map of the local area. It did not escape his attention that the new home was only a handful of miles from the Marine Corps base at Quantico where he had trained so many years ago.

Seventeen

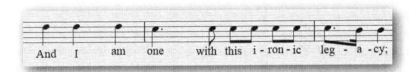

And I am one with this i - ron - ic leg - a -cy;

Frank Jackson Matthews
MARCHE FUNEBRE

J ack paced restlessly back and forth in the small dim-
ly lit gallery. He glanced absentmindedly down at
the tops of his shined shoes and made a small adjust-
ment to the silver clip that held together the ends of his
favorite red and blue striped tie. On the wall to his right
hung a map outlining the major landmarks of the tiny
pacific island of Iwo Jima. On his left a wall size mural
in grainy photographic black and white depicted the
back sides of several Marines charging up a steep dark
sand beach. One of the men carried the tanks of the

heavy flamethrower on his back. A bench, intended as a resting place for weary visitors, sat vacant. All was silent other than the usual recorded sounds of simulated battle noises playing from an unseen speaker. It was one of those rare off-season weekdays when the normally busy gallery was unusually devoid of any guests.

Jack decided it was a good time for a break and wandered quietly through the exhibits toward the front. At the welcome desk sat two young men with high and tight haircuts and freckled faces. "*They look like kids,*" Jack thought to himself as he approached the desk. One of the young men had an obviously wounded arm. The arm reminded Jack that these weren't kids at all…they were Marines; Marines that had already seen action. They were probably only eighteen or nineteen years old; the same age he had been on that fateful trip across the pacific so long ago.

As he approached, one of them looked up from his duty station and called out a friendly greeting, "Hey Frank." Frank…that was a name that Jack had not thought he would answer to again in this lifetime. The young men motioned him over to where they stood behind the expansive marble top desk area with its supply of maps and visitor brochures. One of the boys had a small radio playing. As the octogenarian approached the desk a commercial for a product called "*Extenz®*" began to play. In the first few lines of the advertisement it was made clear that, "*Extenz®*", was a product being promoted as an enhancement to, "*male performance.*" Belying their serious uniformed appearance, the young men adopted goofy grins and began to giggle at the advertisement's content. One of the boys whispered in the other's ear and nudged him a bit with his elbow. With a sly glance and a snicker the second boy said, "Hey Frank...*Extenz®*...is that what you use?"

Without missing a beat, Jack matter-of-factly replied, "No boys...what I use is called *Extinct.*"

The young men erupted in laughter as Jack walked away.

The Marine Corp's "Frank" was now back in action as a volunteer docent for the National Museum of the Marine Corps.

His docent work had begun after a visit to the newly opened museum. Jack was impressed with what he saw. The museum was architecturally stunning with an edifice of gleaming white and glass, the center of which angled sharply into the sky. The design was an interpretation of the iconic photo of five Marines and one Navy Corpsman raising the American flag on Mount Suribachi. It was February 23rd, just five days into the fighting when Marines of the 28th Regiment of the 5th Division climbed to the top of Mount Suribachi and tied a small American flag to a piece of discarded Japanese pipe. Cheers rippled through the American forces and ships horns were heard from the waters surrounding the island. The moment was captured on film by Marine combat photographer, Louis Lowry. That first history making flag proved to be a bit on the small side and, later that same day, a larger flag was sent up the volcano to replace it.

On that afternoon the wind on the mountain whipped, and the men of the 28th pushed hard to get its pole into the air. It was at this precise moment that another photographer, Joe Rosenthal, hurriedly snapped off a couple quick shots and the most famous image from the battle was created. In the years that followed, the flag, and its most famous photographic image, were destined to become the most recognizable symbol not only of the conflict on Iwo Jima, but also of World War II, and of the entire Marine Corps. The very flag depicted in the photo; the flag that once flew over that deadly battle ground in the Pacific, now hung on the wall in the World War II gallery of the museum.

This museum was not the typical dusty repository of historical archives that Jack had expected; it was vibrant and interactive. Within the walls of the 120,000 square foot facility were the very best of modern and technically advanced displays. Lifelike vignettes depicted two hundred years of Marine Corps operations from the Revolutionary War to the War on Terror. Everything from the music and pageantry of the Corps to sobering moments of valor and loss were illustrated.

Jack began to visit the museum more and more often, and it wasn't long before he was asked to be a docent. Jack's normal docent duty station was in the museum's World War II gallery. He stood in the area between a replica of a Higgins boat and the museum's prized display – that famous flag that flew over Mount Suribachi. The Higgins boat replica, which made simulated sounds of the Iwo landings, was an accurate facsimile of the very craft that almost killed him in the waters off of the San Diego coast decades earlier. As the ramp to the boat lowered and visitors exited, Jack was there to greet them and share information about the famous fight for the tiny volcanic island in the Pacific.

Jack's personal stories of being a Marine and his experiences on Iwo were woven into the presentation. Using the map on the gallery wall he would point to various areas of the island and show visitors where he landed on the red beach and hiked to the blue; where the Japanese had stationed their largest guns; and where the Marines had conquered Iwo's critically important air fields. He also told the stories of the ships that had exacted their own revenge. The *USS Tennessee*, the *USS West Virginia*, and the *USS Nevada* might have been downed by the Japanese in the attack on Pearl Harbor, but they weren't out. Those three battle ships

were raised from the shallow harbor in Hawaii and re-
paired to fight again in the Pacific, and most fittingly, to
fight at Iwo Jima. Regardless of which stories he served-
up on a given day, the visitors were always astonished to
find an actual survivor of the battle as their guide into
Iwo history.

It wasn't long after he started volunteering that
he was being asked to do interviews for television and
newspapers, to sit on discussion panels, or be filmed
for historical archives. At first Jack didn't really care
for these interruptions in his day. His visitors experience at the museum was his priority and he saw these
extraneous events as distractions to that duty. Despite
his initial reticence, he always cooperated with the requests. He felt obligated to do so. It was not that he felt
particularly beholden to the journalists or archivists;
He felt obligated to the others, the ones who could not
speak for themselves. He spoke for those veterans who
were now too old or too frail to share their stories, and
for those simply couldn't bear to share them. Most of
all he spoke for the almost 7000 Marines who never
left Iwo. He always looked at it that way. In his mind
many of those guys would have ended up in the higher ranks of the Marines, having distinguished careers
and stars on their chests... he was not a Marine of any
particular accomplishment...just a Private First Class,
nothing more.

Sometimes the requests he received were of a more personal nature. It was one otherwise routine day at the museum when a man came down to the gallery looking for the museum's "Frank." His expression was hopeful as he greeted the docent jovially and shook his hand with a firm grip. The man explained that his company was having a lunch meeting in the rentable space of the museum's cafeteria and he had heard from the staff that there was an Iwo survivor in the building. He was stunned that a World War II veteran would be working, and he had a special question to ask him. The man's father had been killed on Iwo; was there any chance that Jack had known him? Unfortunately, Jack hadn't. The man's father had been assigned to the 25th Regiment and it was doubtful that they had ever crossed paths. The look of disappointment on the man's face was evident. Jack thought for a moment and then said, "If you like I can tell you how he probably spent his last days." He proceeded to show the man where the 25th landed, what their task had been, how they had fought, and how they had given their lives for their brother's, and their country. He offered the man details about his father's last day of life that he would never have known if it were not for this unexpected encounter at the museum. The man was so moved by their talk that he invited the docent to speak to his entire group in the cafeteria that very day and Jack obliged. When he had finished speaking about the sacrifice made by the man's father and the other men of the 25th, he paused and looked around the room. Everyone was in tears… men and women…young and old. Some of the people were openly sobbing, others dabbed at their eyes with tissue. There was not a dry eye in the room.

He hadn't intended to make *anyone* cry, much less *everyone*. In fact he normally tried to make visitors laugh. Jack would always do his best to weave a few jokes into the information he would provide on Iwo Jima. After all, the visitors were usually on vacation and the horror of death and tragedy needed to be balanced a bit with a little whimsy. Plus it was his nature to joke. He took what happened on Iwo Jima very seriously. He took being a Marine seriously. He refused to take himself too seriously. A crowd favorite was when he would point out that the museum had *two genuine artifacts* on display from the island that were actually part of the battle, "the flag… and me." This always produced a round of laughter from the gathering.

While manning his post he was consistently pelted with a variety of questions about World War II. The visitors were a diverse group consisting of all ages and hailing from all parts of the country, and all parts of the world. Their questions were as diverse as they were. Some were about the maps and diagrams on the display walls. Other questions he routinely heard were: "How many Marines died?"

"How many ships were there?"

"How did you get home?"

"Were you wounded?"

Groups of students from high schools would come through on a regular basis, and generally left him wondering about the state of today's educational system. They knew little to nothing about the war, and some of them didn't know the difference between the Atlantic and the Pacific. To them there seemed to be only two places that existed in the world – here, and not here. They knew where they were now, and where they had come from, but nothing more. The questions he heard from the students ranged from the less-than-brilliant, to all together shocking. One such question was, "Did you meet Hitler?" to which Jack sardonically replied, "No, he was on a ski trip that weekend."

One of Jack's favorite parts of his docent role became telling folks the little known story of the *third* flag raised on Iwo, the one that was rarely talked about. As Jack recalled it… "It must have been fourteen or fifteen days after the flag had gone up on Suribachi …"

Jack's patrol group was returning from an already long day of clearing caves and it was still just mid-morning. They had been promised a much needed break to replenish their ammunition and get a few minutes rest before the next patrol began. The men were just setting down their gear and pulling out their canteens when the patrol leader, clearly aggravated, barked out a new order. "Forget your break Marines, we have to go stand in a line so a General can get a picture of another damn flag." Word spread through the ranks that the only three star general present on the island, General Holland M. Smith, had come into fourth division headquarters looking for men to form a Parade line in observance of a flag raising over the Fourth Division cemetery near the base of Mt. Suribachi. Apparently the General, though high in rank, only directly commanded a handful of secretaries and other personnel, and he wanted a large number of Marines to stand at attention for the event. Jack and the others said goodbye to their chance for rest and did as they were told.

They watched at attention as the flag in the cemetery was raised and the flag flying over Mt. Suribachi was lowered. With this action the Admirals and Generals declared that the Japanese claim to the island was officially over and that Iwo Jima was now an American territory. Apparently the Japanese did not share this sentiment because Jack and the rest of the patrol went back to the work of clearing caves and dodging bullets.

Never did it cross Jack's mind on that day in 1945, that thousands of miles away, and seventy years later, he would stand day after day in front of the very flag that had been lowered as he stood at attention in the Fourth

Division cemetery. The eighteen-year-old Marine could not have imagined that in his eighties he would tell its story to soldiers, sailors, American citizens of all ages, and visitors from around the world. Sometimes he wondered why he was the one to stand here and tell these stories. He didn't have the answer to that question. He certainly wasn't the most successful, either in his civilian life or in the Marine Corps. All he knew was that from age eighteen to eighty-nine, this icon of American freedom, this symbolic foe of tyranny and oppression, this woven testament to bravery in the face of insurmountable odds, had wrapped around his life. He felt a certain kinship with the flag, as if it were an old partner from long ago. He and the flag were back together in a different time, and with a different mission. Once upon a time they had each changed history, and now they each told that history.

When he was done recounting the flag story to the last group of visitors, he ushered them on into the adjacent gallery where a different docent was waiting with a different Marine Corps story. It was the end of another day at the museum and Jack walked to the front and said goodnight to the boys closing up at the desk. He was heading for home and there was no time to dawdle.

After all, tonight there was more music to write…

Now, you know Jack.

Epilogue and Acknowledgments

Today, Frank Jackson Matthews continues with his duties as a volunteer docent for the National Museum of the Marine Corps where he is frequently seen welcoming guests into the World War II gallery. He routinely participates in forums, interviews, and filming of his recollections of events during the war. Some of his original music compositions have been played by the Marine Corp's *Band of America's Few,* and are currently being considered by several other professional orchestras for future performance. He has recently retired from privately teaching young piano students after decades of fashioning new generations of piano players and composers. A fact which I think would make Mrs. Crosby Adams particularly proud.

Jack continues to live with youngest daughter, Janet, and son-in-law, Rich, in Stafford Virginia. Their home became a base of operations for Jack and I while working on this book. Both Rich and Janet were welcoming throughout this long process, always giving us space to work, helping dig through boxes of photos and memorabilia, and even opening the occasional bottle of wine as our sessions lingered on into the evening. Jack's elder daughter, Madeline, along with her husband Tom, lives in California and she talks with and visits her father frequently.

Mrs. Crosby Adams passed away while still living at Montreat in 1951 at the age of 93. She is remembered in history as an extraordinarily talented pianist, composer, and teacher. Montreat continues to be a peaceful mountain getaway and conference center affiliated with the Presbyterian Church. In 1942 and 1943 the retreat played its own history-making role in World War II. When war was declared on the Axis powers, many German and Japanese diplomats, consulate staff, and business owners, along with their respective families were living on American soil. These families, including numerous children, were detained at Montreat where they were housed in seclusion and relative comfort. Eventually, the detainees were exchanged for American diplomats and other expatriates being held by Axis powers.

The National Museum of the Marine Corps is an impressive facility that is expanding with the addition of new galleries. They are open to the public 364 days a year from 9am to 5pm. Admission and parking are both free.

The Hotel del Coronado remains a grand and thriving luxury resort on the California Coastline. The 125 year-old hotel is now designated as a National Historical Landmark. The Del staff were especially prompt and gracious in responding to my inquires.

The Lost Colony continues to reenact the history of the first attempt at permanent settlement by English colonists. Each summer thespians take the stage at the Waterside Theater in Manteo, North Carolina and play out the dreams and the drama of a group of colonists whose fate is lost to history. The nearly eighty-year old play is produced by the Roanoke Island Historical Association.

For those of you who like to follow the chronicle of ships, I offer the following:

The USS Sanborn continued her service in World War II throughout the pacific and following the war she was part of *Operation Magic Carpet* which brought troops home from the Pacific Theatre. She served in a number of training exercises during the Korean conflict and worked in the Mediterranean as part of the U.S. 6th Fleet. Back in her home port of Norfolk, Virginia, she had a starring role in the film *Away All Boats* where she can be seen as the *USS Belinda*. She was finally struck from Navy roles in 1960 and scrapped in 1971.

The USS President Polk also participated in *Operation Magic Carpet*. She was returned to her pre-war owner, American President Lines, in 1946. When finally assuming her originally intended role as a commercial cruise ship, she took passengers around the world from port in San Francisco, to Asia, India, the Mediterranean, and back across the Atlantic to New York. She was sold to a private company in Liberia in 1965 and then scrapped in 1970.

The SS Constitution which was built in 1951 and originally ran passenger routes from New York to Europe, was perhaps most famous for transporting Grace Kelly to her wedding to Prince Rainer in Monaco. She was not a camera shy vessel and appeared in film many times including in *An Affair to Remember* with Carey Grant, and in the episode, *All Thieves on Deck*, of the television show *Magnum P.I.* After sailing the Hawaiian Islands route for many years she was sold for scrap but sank while under tow.

I would like to offer my thanks to Cathy Wilhelm, a fellow author who graciously gave me encouragement and publishing advice at just the right moment in time.

I also thank my mother Carol, and my sister, Jennifer, who are voracious readers and who offered two sets of critical eyes.

Most of all I want to thank my husband who made countless trips with me to Virginia and supported this process in more ways than I could list here or even begin to explain.

Winston Churchill once said that, "*Writing a book is an adventure. To begin with, it is a toy and an amusement. Then it becomes a mistress, then it becomes a master, and then it becomes a tyrant. The last phase is that just as you are about to be reconciled to your servitude, you kill the monster and fling him to the public.*" Churchill's appraisal of the writing process is much like I imagine the man himself was; insightful and awfully accurate.

Throughout my work on this book I felt both a sense of intensity and compelling obligation that I could not ascertain the source of. It was undeniably insistent and for that I must humbly acknowledge the hand of God.

Jack and I have always had an easy and natural report, as well as a true affection and appreciation for one another. Jack has both a tremendous memory and the capacity for making us all laugh. His manner of storytelling is engaging and easy to listen to. Many times I found myself so wrapped up in one of his tales that I would forget to take notes and then have to sheepishly request that he start over from the beginning. He always obliged. In the traditional understanding, he is my husband's uncle, but he has never hesitated or equivocated in referring to me as his niece. That never escaped my attention. Real family is not about names on the diagram of a tree. Families are the people who truly care for one another and invest in one another's lives.

Thank You Uncle Jack.

Made in the USA
Lexington, KY
12 April 2016